A Path to Follow

A Path to Follow

LEARNING TO LISTEN TO PARENTS

PATRICIA A. EDWARDS
WITH HEATHER M. PLEASANTS
AND SARAH H. FRANKLIN

HEINEMANN
Portsmouth, NH

The publisher wishes to acknowledge that pp.28-32 were adapted from *Taking Note: Improving Your Observational Notetaking* by Brenda Miller Power, published by Stenhouse. We regret this oversight, and will correct it in subsequent printings.

Heinemann
A division of Reed Elsevier Inc.
361 Hanover Street
Portsmouth, NH 03801–3912
http://www.heinemann.com

Offices and agents throughout the world

© 1999 by Patricia A. Edwards, Heather M. Pleasants, and Sarah H. Franklin

Library of Congress Cataloging-in-Publication Data
Edwards, Patricia A. (Patricia Ann), 1949–
    A path to follow : learning to listen to parents / Patricia A. Edwards with Heather M. Pleasants and Sarah H. Franklin.
        p. cm.
    Includes bibliographical references.
    ISBN 0-325-00152-9
    1. Education, Elementary—Parent participation—United States.   2. Home and school—United States.   I. Pleasants, Heather M.   II. Franklin, Sarah H. 1972– .   III. Title.
    LB1048.5.E39   1999
    372.1103—dc21   98-53451
                                                                                                              CIP

Editor: William Varner
Production service: Patricia Adams
Production coordination: Abigail M. Heim
Cover design: Julie Nelson Gould
Manufacturing: Louise Richardson

Printed in the United States of America on acid-free paper

03 02 01 00 99 DA 1 2 3 4 5

To Annie Kate Edwards, Sharon A. Ransom,
and "Memaw" Griffin,
and in memory of John Edwards

Contents

Acknowledgments

We cannot adequately express our gratitude to the parents and teachers of the schools from which the data in this book is drawn. Without their consistent interest and trust, the project from which this book is derived would not have been possible. It also has been a pleasure to work with them and to be allowed to struggle to understand their lives.

We thank the teachers who took Pat's TE 851 course "Literacy for the Young Child at Home and School," fall 1997 for all of their feedback and suggestions on how to make parent "stories" a highly effective tool for classroom teachers. This group of teachers includes: Joy Pinheiro-Babcock, Mary Katherine Ballard, Claire Blatt, Katherine Hagel-Clarke, Tamara Culver, Wendy Curtis, Susan Henry, Janelle Marler Kamp, Karen Marshall, Connie Pruitt, Tracy Reynolds, Barbara Ripper, Elvy Pearl Rolle, Coretta Smith, Marian Sohn, Tori Steingreaber, Ginny Milbourne Stokes, Karen Summers, and Kelly Thieme.

We thank Catherine Snow and Victoria Purcell-Gates for inviting Pat in December 1993 to deliver a keynote address at the Harvard Graduate School of Education and the Harvard Forum on Schooling and Children entitled "Ready to Learn? Young Children and Their Families." At this conference, Pat shared her pilot data, which involved collecting literacy stories from first-grade parents. We thank two participants who attended the Harvard Forum; Susan Lehr (Skidmore College) and Kelvin Swick (University of South Carolina-Columbia) for inviting Pat to present her pilot data at conferences held at their universities. We also thank the Spencer Foundation and the U.S. Department of Education (Center for the Improvement of Early Reading Improvement) for funding Pat to conduct a more in-depth study of parent stories.

We would like to thank Dr. Jerry Bauch, Professor of Early Childhood, Vanderbilt University, for introducing Sarah to the idea of creating a resource file of community resources. Sarah applied her knowledge and expertise of creating a resource file to model for classroom teachers how this idea could be applied to parent stories.

We would also like to thank Gwendolyn McMillon, who worked on some of the data, and Jo Lesser who offered interesting and useful ideas. We would also like to thank our families and friends who encouraged us through turbulent times and calm, through creative periods and fallow, and generally kept the project alive and gave point and purpose to it all.

We owe much to our editor at Heinemann. William Varner made us believe that we could do this. He provided the utmost in quality, patient editorial assistance, while at the same time supplying an abundance of warmth and friendship. He has enriched our lives, professionally and personally. We are fortunate to have gotten to know him.

Foreword

In 1993, I first heard Pat Edwards talk about the "literacy stories" she had elicited from parents of first and second graders. It was immediately apparent that these stories were an invaluable source of information about the children and their progress toward becoming literate, as well as about the families and their efforts to help. Such information, in the hands of teachers, could provide the basis for productive collaboration with parents to support children's development, and could substantially enrich the portrait of the child sketched from assessments and observations in the classroom.

Parent-teacher collaboration is, of course, the ideal circumstance for helping children learn. But establishing effective communication between parents and teachers is often difficult, for many reasons. In some cases, school personnel make sincere but ineffective efforts to involve parents, then lower expectations and stop trying when those early efforts fail. In some cases, parents believe that academic development is a domain of teacher expertise and responsibility, just as medical care is the responsibility of doctors, and that they themselves should be focusing on moral development. These parents are not shirking their duties—they are simply operating on a view of responsibility that is somewhat different from the school's, and lack the opportunity to revise their view with input from the school. In other cases, both parents and teachers make real efforts to communicate about the children for whom they share responsibility, but the communicative channels are sufficiently noisy that little effective communication results.

Current channels for contact between parents and teachers are, as Edwards, Pleasants, and Franklin so precisely express it, "ritualized and institutionalized"; parent-teacher conferences scheduled for a precise fifteen minutes, scheduled visits to classrooms by all the parents at the same time, report cards and notes sent home—all these are invitations to start a conversation, rather than real opportunities for conversation. If parent-teacher contact is to be informative, it must be open-ended, flexible, reciprocal, responsive to topics of individual interest, mutually constructed, and richly contextualized. The institutionalized contact most schools provide for must be supplemented by additional and alternative channels of communication. In this book, Edwards, Pleasants, and Franklin provide such an alternative.

A Path to Follow is predicated on the observation that stories constitute the best vehicle for organizing and conveying psychological knowledge—knowledge about people and their goals, motives, strategies, accomplishments, and difficulties. Stories about children's reading and writing show them struggling, learning, sometimes failing, sometimes triumphing, and very often getting help from the adults in their families. Stories about children's literacy are also stories about the families' goals, motives, strategies, accomplishments, difficulties, and engagement with literacy. These stories thus reveal a degree of familial commitment to children's school achievement that teachers need to hear about, and provide insight about the children and their families that teachers might never have access to any other way.

Family stories are not, of course, the only source of information teachers need about children. Tests provide scores, observations in classrooms provide notebook entries, tasks of reading and writing provide skill estimates. All these facts about children are correct, informative, and helpful. But the stories parents tell about children carry a much more complex truth. We need to hear them.

The authors' work reveals them as idealists—as people who believe that teachers and parents can work together to improve schooling outcomes for children. But they are very practical idealists—educators who understand how to provide the tools that will bring the ideal of parent-teacher collaboration within reach. Thus, while the impulse for this book was deeply idealistic, the book itself is eminently practical—it is a detailed guide for educators interested in doing a better job, and a model for parents of how they might improve their communication with their children's teachers. It should also be read by educational administrators, who need to understand that establishing effective contact and productive collaboration between parents and schools requires more than a ritual, and is not a frill but an absolute requirement. Schools must redefine their responsibilities to ensure that such collaboration is established. *A Path to Follow* is a perfect place to start.

Catherine Snow

Introduction

This is a book that directly addresses one of the toughest issues facing today's schools—parental involvement. Educators have never had a better or more challenging opportunity to explore how to involve parents in the educational support of their children. The importance of parental involvement is acknowledged in the vision and mission statements of schools and school charters (McGilp and Michael, 1994). "Home and school should work together" is the refrain heard again and again, along with the mantra that parents must let their children know they care about education and support what the schools are doing.

Teachers across the country emphasize that parents should encourage their children to work hard, read with them at home, ask about their school day, visit the school, and talk to teachers. At the same time, we are told that children do better in school if parents do "their part" at home. Like others, we have found that building effective links between home and school is far from easy. PTA meetings, parent-teacher conferences, and yearly open houses are not enough—and usually are not well enough attended—to ensure adequate communication. Many parents remain completely isolated from the schools, because they have been alienated from schools in the past, or perceive themselves as not having enough time and opportunity.

Despite this reality, superintendents, principals, and teachers still pursue creating a closer working relationship with parents and continue to make the following request: "I want parents involved in the educational development of their children." Obviously, educators mean what they say. Unfortunately, many have not been as successful as they would like in their attempts to reach out to families and incorporate them in the educational process. Even when educators have reached out to families, often their efforts have been superficial and ineffective.

As authors of this book, we are unwilling to accept that parental involvement is simply "something" that virtually everybody wants, but is unattainable. We firmly believe that teachers are professionals who can master the challenge of working with and relating to families, not just children. Unfortunately, there are few guidelines or standards for teachers as they attempt to involve the whole family in a child's education. This contrasts with other professions in the United States, starting with medicine, and continuing through law, architecture, engineering, and nursing that are characterized by a specialized knowledge base, a commitment to client welfare, and the definition and transmission of professional standards (Darling-Hammond and Cobb, 1996).

Fortunately, it seems that the teaching profession is changing, and a consensus is developing about what teachers should know and be able to do. In recent years, professional associations like the Holmes Group, the American Association of Colleges for Teacher Education, and the Association of Teacher Educators have worked to define a common core of ideas and experiences for teacher education. All of these groups have articulated a view of teaching knowledge, skills, and dispositions which emphasizes that:

- Teachers should strive to create successful learners from a pool of children who come from various backgrounds and preparations.
- Teachers should facilitate the development of the whole child.
- Teachers should employ their own cumulative life and professional experiences.
- Teachers should be professionally reflective.

Despite the consensus among professional organizations, there is much less commonality in actual practice. It is unfortunate there is no mechanism in place for teachers to respond to the common core of understanding that characterizes what all teachers need to know and be able to do to address the individual needs of all children.

With this book, we suggest that parent stories could be one tool for teachers to draw on when they seek to involve parents in their child's education. It is a common practice for professionals like doctors, lawyers, and architects to collect information, which gives them particular insights about their patients/clients. Teachers are often criticized for not living in the neighborhoods in which they teach, but rarely do doctors, lawyers, or architects live in the neighborhoods in which they practice their professional craft. Instead these professionals rely on collecting information as a way of developing a professional interaction with their patients/clients. We approach parent involvement in the same way.

We approach parent involvement in this manner because we recognize that most teachers, schools, and families admit to a lack of communication. When and how did schools and families diverge? Over the course of time, communities and, thereby, schools have become increasingly fragmented. Parents, schools, and the communities that serve both have lost sight of each other and the responsibilities each hold. The American education system serves children for 13 years in the public schools, longer if children attend preschool or day care programs. Presently, communication with parents occurs only a few times per year on an individual basis and probably even less often on a group/social platform. A child's future hangs in this precarious balance.

In addition, schools may be very separate from the communities in which the children live. Society itself has become less nuclear and communal. Many households are run by single parents. The extended family may live hundreds of miles apart, weakening support systems for families with young children. The economy dictates that more households operate on two incomes, leaving less time for parents to be involved in a child's general needs. Because of these social, political, and logistical issues, teachers and schools find themselves increasingly disconnected from communities and parents.

Without the support of those two pivotal systems, schools have become overburdened and have lost both the insight and ability to accomplish their original goal, to teach. Indeed, "the diverse and difficult needs of today's youth far exceed the ability of any single institution to meet them. Recognition of this fact has fueled policies that encourage or require strategies such as 'integrated services,' 'interagency collaboration,' 'co-located or school-linked services,' or 'school-community partnerships'" (Heath and McLaughlin, 1996, p. 69).

Realizing that schools and families do not communicate effectively prompts the need to regroup and work together to meet the needs of America's children. How can schools begin to instigate better systems of gathering and sharing information from/with parents? In order to construct the two-way communication necessary to build the groundwork for "parent stories" to evolve, schools, teachers, and parents must enter a partnership not unlike an arranged marriage. Trust must be developed in order to gain maximum information. Through the use of parent stories, we hope that trust will begin to develop between teachers and parents.

WHAT ARE PARENT STORIES?

According to Vandergrift and Greene (1992) "every parent has his or her own story to tell" (p. 57). Coles (1989) further contends that "one's responses to a story is just as revealing as the story itself" (p. 18). We define parent "stories" as the narratives gained from open-ended conversations and/or interviews. In these interviews, parents respond to questions designed to provide information about traditional and nontraditional early literacy activities and experiences that have happened in the home. We also define parent stories through their ability to construct home literacy environments for teachers, and by their ability to connect home and school. By using stories as a way to express the nature of the home environment, parents can select anecdotes and personal observations from their own individual consciousness to give teachers access to complicated social, emotional, and educational issues that can help teachers unravel the mystery around their students' early literacy beginnings.

Many parents have vivid memories of their children's early development; specific interactions they had with their children; observations of their children's beginning learning efforts; ways in which their children learned; perceptions as to whether their occupation determined how they raised their children; descriptions of "teachable moments" they had with their children; and descriptions of things about their children that may not be obvious to the teacher but would help their children's performance if the teacher knew.

Parent stories can provide teachers with the opportunity to gain a deeper understanding of the "human side" of families and children (i.e., why children behave as they do, children's ways of learning and communicating, some of the problems parents have encountered, and how these problems may have impacted their children's views about school and the schooling process).

WHY IS IT NECESSARY TO LEARN ABOUT THE "HUMAN SIDE" OF FAMILIES AND CHILDREN?

Teachers and families need to explore each other's beliefs and ideas about who is responsible for what elements of the child's development. For instance, many parents see their formal educational role ceasing when their child enters kindergarten. However, by ignoring alternative views to education, teachers set themselves up for hostility from parents and the public who believe that the institution has shortchanged their child/children. Indeed schools and teachers have fallen short by failing to communicate their own expectations, listen to parents' expectations, and to mutually define and delegate responsibilities in this partnership.

In order to ensure educational success for the majority of children, communication reform and partnership development through parent stories need to address four issues: (1) families and children face great individual and social pressures, all of which we may not know or understand; (2) schools and teachers need to instigate open communication that occurs *between* families and schools *not from* schools *to* families; (3) schools and teachers must recognize their own strengths and limitations and delegate responsibility for issues outside of their expertise; (4) and teachers and schools need to develop "multiple consciousness" in order to maintain plurality in society while also striving for unity to foster educational success in the classroom.

⋋ Schools and teachers must realize that children do not live in a utopia free of the problems that plague adults. Children are a part of society, and what happens in their family, community, and school affects them and all aspects of their development (see Figure 1—a series of concentric circles with the child in the innermost circle then family, neighborhood, school, community, district, town/city, state, region, nation, world).

One must also realize that children who are at risk come from all SES levels, educational attainment, religions, races, and genders. While most of the parent stories we include in this book come from predominantly low SES families, there are many children who come from middle-class and affluent families who may suffer from abuse and neglect. Schools must be careful not to discriminate against children based on how they are clothed, what neighborhood they live in, or who their parents are and what they do. All families should be treated equally and offered unbiased, open, two-way communication with teachers and school officials. In other words, parent stories should

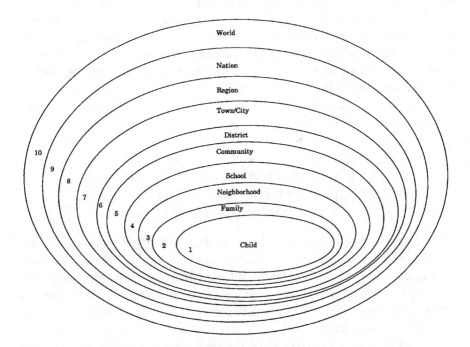

Figure 1. Social World of Children

occur with all parents, not just with parents whose children are labeled "at risk" based on how they look or on their academic performance.

When gathering information from children and families through observation and parent stories, the schools must be careful to engage in equal conversations. Often schools and teachers take a "father-knows-best" approach; essentially parenting the parent. Schools must realize that while they may have expertise on pedagogy, curriculum, and child development, they are not experts on individual families or children. The parents know their child and what occurs in their family better than any outsider and schools/teachers need to respect and learn from their clientele. It is especially important in listening to parents as they tell their stories to simply collect the information and analyze it to match potential needs with available resources, not to pass moral, political, or personal judgment on what they are saying. Doing so could risk permanently closing off current and future communication efforts.

Du Bois (1990) wrote of the plight of African Americans prior to desegregation. He commented that the white person need only be conscious of what it was like to be white, a life without restrictions based on race. However, black men and women needed to have what he called a "double-consciousness," to know what it was to be black and know the associated limitations, but also to know the life of white people as different and less limiting than their own.

In twentieth century, broadly diverse American culture, teachers need to employ a multiple consciousness. Upon entering the classroom, one can guarantee that all children in any given classroom *do not* have identical racial, ethnic, religious, social, educational, or financial backgrounds to the teacher. Teachers must learn from parents' stories in order to gain a better sense of who the children are and expand their own schema to encompass an increasingly diverse society and classroom.

RESEARCH SUPPORT FOR USING PARENT STORIES TO UNDERSTAND AND INVOLVE FAMILIES

According to Danridge (1998), "The heart of schooling beats in the classroom. It is the place where students and teachers interact" (p. 1). If the way we teach is guided by the needs of developing children, then it will not only reshape our classroom *practice,* it will reshape our classroom *environment.* The classroom acts as a kind of *aquarium,* reflecting the ideas, ethics, attitudes, and life of the people who live in it.

Looking into the aquarium, we often believe that the reality of life within it is plainly obvious. What we fail to realize is that there can be many types of "fish" within an aquarium and not all are equally equipped to survive in the environment that is prepared for them. If teachers don't know how to change the environment in which students "swim," then that becomes problematic for the students, the teacher, and ultimately the parents.

All too often the classroom fails to act as a successful aquarium. In Chapter One we identity some "cultural variables" that contribute to the home and school being compatible or incompatible with each other—*social organization, sociolinguistics, cognition, and motivation* (see Tharp, 1989). We also identify four areas of potential cultural conflict: *learning style, interactional or relational style, communication, and differing perceptions of involvement* (see Gilbert and Gay, 1985). We suggest that what teachers need to do now is to consider these "cultural variables" in conjunction with the potential areas of conflict. *That is, they need to think more about how particular ways of living, communicating, and thinking effect learning, interactions, and perceptions.*

Over the years, researchers have continued to examine these issues (Au and Jordan, 1981, Au and Kawakami, 1994, Hale-Benson, 1982, Nieto, 1996, Ladson-Billings, 1995). For example, those within the multicultural education movement have attempted to enhance learning and achievement by promoting understanding about cultural differences within the classroom.

One concept that came out of this movement is *cultural responsiveness.* Over the years, terms such as culturally relevant, culturally compatible, and culturally appropriate have been used interchangeably and have much in common (Au and Kawakami, 1994). The commonality among these terms is that they focus on understanding the culture of students and their families and how this knowledge could be utilized in the classroom. In this discussion, we will use the term *culturally responsive.* Cultural responsiveness is first based upon a premise that schools and classrooms have a culture of power that values specific ways of behaving, thinking, and learning. Secondly, culturally responsive teachers learn about the cultural-specific traits of their students and use them as guidelines for understanding and teaching (Shade, Kelly, and Oberg, 1997). Ladson-Billings (1994) reported that these kinds of teachers showed their students that they care about what they taught them; their lessons were personally relevant to the students' lives as well as their own. Furthermore, these teachers demonstrated their value of knowledge by talking openly with the students about how their learning affected their lives. They connected new concepts and facts to current events, community and social issues, and the like. Finally, these teachers had a deep conviction and commitment to teaching because they conceptualized knowledge as a powerful socially constructed tool.

It is important to mention that being culturally responsive does not mean that teachers must be of the same racial/ethnic heritage of their students in order to be effective. Cultural similarities between students and teachers (i.e., African American teachers teaching African American students) should not be assumed to underlie culturally responsive teaching because not all minority (African American, Hispanic, Asian) teachers are culturally responsive. Ladson-Billings interviewed eight successful teachers of African American children, and three of them were white. She argued that the individual idiosyncrasies of these teachers (i.e, race/culture, age, teaching style) were not as important as the ways in which these teachers interpersonally related to their students and facilitated their learning. What we found interesting about the research relating to culturally responsive teaching is that researchers have spent a great deal of time describing what culturally responsive teachers do, but have failed to reveal how teachers become culturally responsive. We applaud this work, but we know that becoming a culturally responsive teacher is not something magical. Additionally, this research has not enhanced our knowledge about families and it is not drawing on what we know about which "cultural variables" cause the most "trouble" for teachers who are unaware of the home literacy environments of their students.

Time after time, the research literature has revealed what occurs when teachers do not know how to utilize the home literacy environments of their students. Phelan, Davidson and Cao (1991) reported that students did reasonably well academically with teachers who tried to adapt their teaching to the students' ways of learning and interacting outside of school. They found that when forced to choose between the peer group and the school, or between home and school, many students did not choose school and consequently failed. For example, Trueba (1989) described immigrant children who were unable to comprehend classroom instruction or who responded to the teacher in a way different from that which the teacher expected. Over time, the children's academic performance dropped, as did their effort. Although teachers viewed the students as exhibiting learning disabilities, Trueba argued that the students' learning abilities were normal, but that the culture of the classroom was sufficiently different from the home culture as to make it impossible for them to function well. Expressing the stress of repeated failure, the students stopped trying. In another example, Jordan (1985) and her colleagues identified key practices that were interfering with native Hawaiian children's learning. Hawaiian children spend considerable time working with peers outside of school; if they are punished for interacting with peers in the classroom, and especially if punishment involves isolating them, they will put their energy into establishing illicit contact with peers. If a moderate level of peer interaction is allowed, they tend to stay on task.

Literacy is a broad term, and the school is a particularly crucial institution for mediating the process by which the individual becomes literate or in reflecting societal views of what constitutes literacy (Ferdman, 1991). Roth (1984) put it this way:

> Social/cultural control is tied directly to the structure of knowledge and to the manner in which knowledge is presented in the schooling context. Schools, acting as agents for the culture, control the extent to which personal knowledge may enter into the public knowledge of school curriculum; they thus have a direct influence upon cultural continuity and change. In selecting what to teach and how it is to be taught and evaluated, schools reaffirm what the culture values as knowledge . . . (p. 303).

Roth acknowledged the "potential cultural conflicts" in the structure and presentation of knowledge. She highlighted controls placed on cultural variables that might enter school curriculum through the "personal knowledge" students from different cultures bring to the classroom. Too often teachers focus on large or historical cultural traditions in their classrooms and fail to consider the personal knowledge of students that accompanies those traditions. Therefore, we offer parent stories as a mechanism for helping teachers consider the *personal knowledge* of families and children.

THE IMPORTANCE OF LISTENING TO PARENT STORIES

In her book *Composing a Life*, Mary Catherine Bateson (1990), suggests that a commonly held assumption—that people's lives progress in single and unwavering lines toward specific goals—is rarely true for most people. She argues instead that we craft our lives, just as painters or poets or musicians craft their works of art, by bringing together various elements and experiences, shaping them to fit our visions, and forming them into a coherent whole. We feel that if teachers were to allow able parents to act like skilled novelists, parents would create stories, and it is through these stories that parents would be able to incorporate even seemingly unconnected bits and pieces about their children into a cohesive literacy life story. And, since the process of composing a life is ongoing, and requires, a "continual reimagining of the future and reinterpretation of the past to give meaning to the present" (Bateson, 1990, p. 29), parent stories are ever-evolving. Metzger (1986) has offered a similar analysis of why stories are a useful way for parents to share information with the teacher about their child. Metzger observed that:

> Stories go in circles. They don't go in straight lines. So it helps if you listen in circles because there are stories inside stories and stories between stories

and finding your way through them is as easy and hard as finding your way home. And part of the finding is the getting lost. If you're lost, you really start to look around and listen (p. 104).

We feel that inviting parents to tell their stories will in turn invite and encourage teachers to really listen to parents in the way that Metzger has described. Inviting parents to tell their stories shifts the order of relationship between teachers and parents. Parents become the "more knowledgeable other" about their child especially when it comes to interpreting and describing their child's home environment and the role they play in preparing their child for school. Through the telling of these stories, parents are recognized (whether they are literate or not) as "experts" in describing and interpreting methods and codes used in their home literacy environment which may be invisible to teachers. This is especially important given the perspective that parents and school teachers are a child's first and second most important teachers— parents must have the opportunity to give teachers personal information that may help teachers to understand how children can best learn in their classrooms. All of the parents do not hold answers to their children's literacy problems, neither do teachers—but by combining the knowledge of both of these groups of people, we will have a more complete picture of children's home and school lives.

As stated earlier, the collection of parent stories is one possible way that a dialogue between parents and teachers can be initiated. Parents have more control over what they are saying in parent stories, even though it is still sensitive information. However, there must be explicit understandings between the teacher and parents about how these records can be used, and teachers and parents must agree that the information parents provide will be used for the benefit of students.

We understand that some of the information from parent stories may be viewed as negative or counterproductive to the education of the children. However, we argue that parent stories reflect the realities of many school children that grow up in what is typically described as at-risk environments; these realities must be confronted and dealt with. Teachers may feel that they have minimal control over what happens in the home and virtually no specialized training to uncloset parent stories. Teachers may also feel that they are crossing the boundaries of families' right to privacy if they attempt to talk with parents about the home environments of students. However, if teachers are to educate all children, they must begin to think about ways to help the children in their classrooms become "ready to learn," and they must receive training and preparation for dealing with the issues that children bring to school with them.

Our book is divided into five chapters. In Chapter One, "Mapping the Terrain," we focus initially on discussing why parents and teachers have not become the partners that we would like them to be. Next, we summarize the literature, which has uncovered aspects of home and school literacies. We present this work as part of a very important puzzle. Lastly, we use this chapter to introduce parent stories, as a path to follow.

In Chapter Two, "At-Risk Students and Parental Involvement," we include teachers' descriptions of at-risk students and we consider the difficulties of establishing conversations with the parents of these students.

In Chapter Three, "Collecting Parent Stories," we discuss the kind of questions that teachers have asked in the past and make the case that those questions were one-dimensional. We then introduce the context, which led to the development of our interview questionnaire. We share the interview questionnaire and how classroom teachers could adapt it.

In Chapter Four, "Making Sense of Parent Stories," we walk through the process of extrapolating salient information from conversations based on parent interviews. We also provide an action plan that teachers can use to guide further conversations with parents and to develop instructional plans for students.

In Chapter Five, "Implications of Parent Stories," we discuss how teachers can seek help and referrals outside the school by creating a resource file. We draw on a parent story narrative to discuss what agencies and organizations teachers can access when students' difficulties are beyond their control and expertise.

POSSIBLE AUDIENCES AND USES FOR THE BOOK

In the process of preparing to write this book, we had many conversations about the importance of a book such as this, and who might be interested in reading the words of parents as they are given here. We see this book as useful for all who are interested in exploring the voices of those parents who are least often heard from or considered when it comes to understanding the home environments of children, and how this affects school performance.

Teachers

Teachers may find this book useful in a number of ways. Initially, they may be able to identify parent stories, which seem very similar to the stories that are offered by the parents of their own students. Secondly, teachers can use this book as a guide to interview parents of students, and may want to ask the same questions during interview sessions. Parent stories can provide an avenue for networking with parents who may have concerns, questions, or suggestions for teachers. Lastly, with the knowledge provided by interviews like those used in this book, teachers could provide helpful resources for parents and students to use.

Teacher Educators

Teacher educators can use this book to encourage future teachers to value parents as important players on decision-making teams, which determine the students' educational direction. Additionally, this book may be useful in helping teacher educators make students familiar with some of the characteristics that might be present in the children they will teach, and in the parents with whom they will interact. With this knowledge, they will become better prepared to foster positive communication with parents and to understand how to best reach all of their students.

Education Students

Our book can be used to challenge future teachers to build relationships with their students' parents; this relationship could determine the success or failure of a student. For example, education students can role play with other students during their teacher-training period in order to practice interviewing and talking with parents.

Parents

PTA groups, parent support groups, and those that teach parenting classes can begin to understand how past experiences and the home environment can impact children in positive and negative ways in their educational experiences. Parents should be able to read the parent stories and see the similarities and differences in their own lives. Many parents could benefit from knowing that they are not alone in their efforts to help their child or children have better school experiences.

Child-Care Professionals

Child-care professionals might be placed in a better position to determine what kinds of activities and interactions would be most beneficial to children in order to prepare them for academic and social success in school.

Administrators

With knowledge gained from the parent stories presented here, administrators can better encourage home-school network building to increase test scores, to increase volunteerism, and to gain benefits that would occur if parents become understood and fully valued by teachers and the school.

Policymakers

Through development of the ideas conveyed in this book, money could be made available for remedial programs, early childhood programs, and early intervention and prevention programs. Additionally, it is also extremely important for programs to be funded that promote family literacy, parent education, and improvement of the quality of life for all students.

Researchers

It is clear that researchers must do work that makes this kind of information more available to improve the lives of parents as well as students. Students cannot focus on learning if their basic needs are not being met. Books such as ours challenge researchers to remember those who have not been given a voice in all forms of research.

FINAL COMMENTS IN SUPPORT OF PARENT STORIES

Parent stories allow teachers to identify what it means, specifically, when we use the words "home literacy environment" to talk about students' success or lack of success in school. By using parent stories in this way, teachers are able to look at specific issues, problems, and strengths of homes, which influence the literacy development of students. This is the first step towards making connections between parent stories and how they can be used to better educate every child.

Also, parent stories have the potential to alter teacher's own dispositions and practice. The concept of parent stories is supported by work of Taylor and Dorsey-Gaines (1988): "If we are to teach, we must first examine our own assumptions about families and children and we must be alert to the negative images in the literature. . . . Instead of responding to 'pathologies,' we must recognize that what we see may actually be healthy adaptations to an uncertain and stressful world. As teachers, researchers, and policymakers, we need to think about the children themselves and try to imagine the contextual worlds of their day-to-day lives" (p. 203).

In our opinion, parent stories should prompt the investigation and redirection of current "parent-involvement", "parent-teacher communication", and "creation of home-school connections" initiatives. It is also our opinion that parent stories underscore the importance that society must begin to really listen to all parent voices and value their information about their children without prejudice, judgment, or apathy. If we can do this, we will embrace the multiplicity of experiences that parents have and can bring to the educational adventures of their children.

REFERENCES

American Association of Colleges for Teacher Education. 1987. *Teaching Teachers: Facts and Figures (RATE 1)*. Washington, DC: American Association of Colleges for Teacher Education.

American Association of Colleges for Teacher Education. 1987. *Teaching Teachers: Facts and Figures (RATE 11)*. Washington, DC: American Association of Colleges for Teacher Education.

Au, K., and A. J. Kawakami. 1994. "Cultural congruence in instruction." In *Teaching Diverse Populations: Formulating a Knowledge Base*, ed. E. Hollins, J. King, and W. Hayman, 1–23. Albany, NY: State University of New York Press.

Bateson, M. C. 1989. *Composing a Life*. New York: A Plume Book.

Carnegie Task Force on Teaching as a Profession. 1986. *A Nation Prepared Teachers for the Twenty-First Century*. New York: Carnegie Forum on Education and the Economy.

Coles, R. 1989. *The Call of Stories*. Boston: Houghton Mifflin.

Crowson, R. L. 1992. *School-Community Relations, Under Reform*. Berkeley, CA: McCutchan Publishing Corporation.

Danridge, J. 1998. *Culturally Responsive Literacy Pedagogy and Student Motivation*. Unpublished paper, East Lansing, MI: Michigan State University.

Darling-Hammond, L., and V. L. Cobb. 1996. "The Changing Context of Teacher Education." In *The Teacher Educator's Handbook: Building a Knowledge Base for the Preparation of Teachers*, ed. F. B. Murray, 14–62. San Francisco: Jossey-Bass Publishers.

Du Bois, W. E. B. 1990. *The Souls of Black Folk*. New York: Vintage Books/The Library of America.

Ferdman, B. 1991. "Becoming Literate in a Multicultural Society." In *Literate Systems and Individuals Lives: Perspectives on Literacy and Schooling*, ed. E. Jennings and A. Purves, 95–115. Albany, NY: SUNY Press.

Gilbert, S. E., and G. Gay. 1985. "Improving the Success in School of Poor Black Children." *Phi Delta Kappan, 67*(2): 133–137.

Hale-Benson, J. 1982. *Black Children: Their Roots, Their Culture, and Their Learning Styles*. Provo, UT: Brigham Young University Press.

Heath, S. B., and M. W. McLaughlin. 1996. "The Best of Both Worlds: Connecting Schools and Community Youth Organizations for All-Day, All-Year Learning." In *Coordination Among Schools, Families, and Communities: Prospects for Educational Reform*, ed. J. G. Cibulka and W. J. Kritek, 69–93. Albany, NY: University of New York Press.

Holmes Group. 1986. *Tomorrow's Teachers: A Report of the Holmes Group*. East Lansing, MI: Holmes Group.

Jordan, C. 1985. "Translating Culture: From Ethnographic Information to Education Program." *Anthropology and Education Quarterly*, 16: 105–123.

Kaestle, C. F. 1983. *Pillars of the Republic: Common Schools and American Society, 1780–1860*. New York: Hill and Wang.

Ladson-Billings, G. 1994. *The Dreamkeepers: Successful Teachers of African American Children*. San Francisco, CA: Jossey-Bass.

Metzger, D. 1986. "Circles of Stories." Parabola IV (4): Original work published 1969.

McGilp, J., and M. Michael. 1994. *The Home-School Connection: Guidelines for Working with Parents*. Portsmouth, NH: Heinemann.

Nieto, S. 1996. *Affirming Diversity: The Sociopolitical Context of Multicultural Education*. Second edition. New York: Longman.

Phelan, P., A. L. Davidson, and H. T. Cao. 1991. "Student Multiple Worlds: Negotiating the Boundaries of Family, Peers, and School Cultures." *Anthropology and Education Quarterly* 22(3): 224–250.

Roth, R. 1984. "Schooling, Literacy Acquisition and Cultural Transmission." *Journal of Education* 166(3): 291–308.

Shade, B. J., C. Kelly, and M. Oberg. 1997. *Creating Culturally Responsive Classrooms.* Washington, DC: American Psychological Association.

Taylor, D., and C. Dorsey-Gaines. 1988. *Growing Up Literate: Learning from Inner-City Families.* Portsmouth, NH: Heinemann.

Tharp, R. G. 1989. "Psychocultural Variables and Constants: Effects on Teaching and Learning in Schools." *American Psychologist* 44(2): 349–359.

Trueba, H. T. 1989. *Raising Silent Voices: Educating the Linguistic Minorities for the 21st Century.* New York: Newbury House.

Vandergrift, J. A., and A. L. Greene. 1992. "Rethinking Parent Involvement." *Educational Leadership* 50(1): 57–59.

A Path to Follow

1

Mapping the Terrain

He who chooses the beginning of a road chooses the place it leads to.

It is the means that determines the end.

—Harry Emerson Fosdick

B y now you are thinking to yourself that the parent stories idea sounds interesting and that parental involvement is a good thing. With all of the cultural differences, however, such as increasing poverty and generations of individuals in poverty, and the many new immigrants from non-Western cultures attending U.S. schools, there is no way for me as a teacher to really get to know the parents of the children that I teach, even though I know that it would be nice for me to know this information. Some of you are also probably thinking, "I teach in schools where the families and children do not share cultural backgrounds similar to my own." Some of you are probably saying, "I'm not sure I want to delve into the cultural backgrounds of families and children because it is uncharted territory, makes me nervous, and I have mixed feelings."

Well, more than twenty years ago, Sara Lawrence Lightfoot (1978) reported that home-school relationships extending from colonial times to the present have been characterized by relationships that are "worlds apart." While Lightfoot recognized the conflict that exists between these two systems [home and school], she clearly articulates the importance of the home-school connection:

> If [we] recognize the initial social and cultural task assumed by all families and their primary educative function, then it becomes clear that in order for schools to be productive and comfortable environments for children, they will have to meaningfully incorporate the familial and cultural skills and values learned in homes and communities . . . When schools and families support dissonant values and goals, and when families and communities are perceived as inadequate and chaotic environments by arrogant and

threatened school personnel, then education within families is devalued and systematically excluded from the school culture. Children experience the cultural dissonance between home and school, recognize the sharp contrasts and the forced choice they must make for successful accommodation in both worlds, and develop more or less functional strategies for relieving the environmental tensions (pp. 170–171).

In response to Lightfoot's observation, Susan Swap (1992) notes that "We seem suddenly to be in a world where these sharp contrasts and forced choices on cultural differences are more dramatic and frequent . . . One solution to this discontinuity is to recruit more teachers into the school who reflect and value the child's culture. This goal must be a national priority in teacher preparation institutions" (p. 62).

We believe that another solution is to create the opportunity for teachers irrespective of their race, creed, gender, or national origin to understand the families of the children that they teach. Even though teachers might not share the cultures of their students they should be provided with the opportunity to learn about the similarities and differences in their cultures and the cultures of the children and families. This last solution has received strong support from the Clinton administration, as evidenced by the goal to be reached by year 2000 that, "all schools should be ready for children and their families." This goal must be set and met by schools at all grade levels, not just schools for very young children. Schools must inform and involve all families, including those with different cultural backgrounds, to gain their ideas and assistance in helping all children succeed in school.

With the year 2000 only one year away, the question remains "why are schools struggling to accomplish this goal?" Swap (1993) offers some insight. She argues that:

> In theory, parents and teachers agree on the importance of parent involvement and home-school partnership. . . . One would think that with both teachers and parents supporting the principle of home-school partnership and with data confirming its benefits such programs would be universal — or at least commonplace. The paradox is that parent involvement in the schools is surprisingly minimal. (p. 13).

In this chapter, we attempt to map the terrain for understanding the context for parent stories. In the first section we offer some explanations as to why parent involvement is minimal and ambiguous. In the second section we highlight researchers' descriptions, interpretations, observations, and assumptions about the home literacy environments' of families and children. In the final section we build the case that parent stories are a path for understanding families and children.

LOOKING AT THE POLICY
AND RESEARCH

Since the mid-1970s, a growing literature has explored the complicated and often conflict-ridden relationship between schools and parents. While Coleman *et al.* (1966) sparked a good deal of controversy about the relative effects of home and school on children's school achievement, it was several years before scholars began to see the *interactions* between home and school as important in their own right. The findings of nearly thirty years of research suggest a degree of consensus on a number of issues, not all of which are completely consistent with one another:

1. Parent involvement matters for any kind of school program success and for any individual child's school achievement, especially in reading and language arts.

On this point, the consensus extends beyond the research community into the ranks of practitioners, policy makers, and parents themselves. The common wisdom suggests that schools work better when parents are actively "involved" in their children's education, both at home and in the school building. The general importance of parental involvement is accepted without question; behind virtually every PTA meeting, parent-teacher conference, open house, and "know your school night" there is the presumption that parent participation enhances education. Fullan (1982, p. 93) states simply that "emerging from [the] research [on parent and community involvement] in schools is a message which is remarkable in its consistency: the closer the parent is to the education of the child, the greater the impact on child development and educational achievement." When educators talk about parents, both publicly and privately, they concur with Fullan's conclusion.

2. Teachers hold strong and usually negative views about the attitudes of poor, minority, and immigrant parents toward schooling and the school.

In their detailed case study of four elementary school teachers, Carew and Lightfoot (1979) observe that teachers' beliefs are intense and persistent, and that these beliefs are reinforced by the scarce opportunity they have to communicate with parents. According to this research, the relationship teachers are able to have with parents provides little to counter the negative image teachers sometimes hold of parents who are poor, minority, and recent immigrants.

3. Contacts between teachers and parents do not help teachers learn about parents' real attitudes toward schooling, even though they believe parent involvement is so important.

Fullan has described at length the barriers that prevent teachers from learning about the "subjective world of parents" and capitalizing on what parents have to offer (1982, p. 203). Lightfoot (1978) has noted the lack of meaningful contacts between teachers and parents—contacts that would give teachers insight into the kinds of educational attitudes that poor, minority, and recent immigrant parents really hold. Unfortunately, the opinions of teachers about extra-school influences seem to be based on a set of preconceptions rather than on a series of authentic encounters. Lightfoot (1978) observes:

> There are very few opportunities for parents and teachers to come together for meaningful, substantive discussion. In fact, schools organize public, ritualistic occasions that do not allow for real contact, negotiation, or criticism between parents and teachers. Rather, they are institutionalized ways of establishing boundaries between insiders (teachers) and interlopers (parents) under the guise of polite conversation and mature cooperation (pp. 27–29).

On those few occasions that teachers have an opportunity to have a substantive conversation with parents, Lightfoot notes that frustration and hostility seems to occur more frequently than cooperation and mutual accord:

> Teachers rarely call in praise of a child. Usually when parents are summoned to the school, the teacher is reporting on some trouble their child is having . . . Parents, on the other hand, rarely call a teacher to praise her. . . . Whether the contact is initiated by teachers or parents, it becomes a highly charged, defensive interaction (pp. 28–29).

Given these obstacles to meaningful communication, the presumed importance of the family educational context seems only to be matched by how much teachers have yet to understand about how to learn about these contexts. One thing remains consistent and clear: Our main opportunities to evaluate family influences exist through the medium of school-bound teacher-parent interactions.

Given these three findings, the fourth is not surprising.

4. In many cases, the teacher's success in involving parents in school programs has been only minimally successful.

On the one hand, teachers do a number of things to encourage parent involvement with their children's education. Report cards, conferences, newsletters, and open houses are a regular part of the school year. On the other hand, teachers are very much aware of the extent to which parent involvement can increase the professional uncertainty they confront in the classrooms. Lortie's observations (1975, p. 189) suggest that teachers are vulnerable both to parent complaints and to parent "assistance." Teachers work hard to "build and sustain a social order [in the classroom] with people over whom they have only limited, place-bound authority," and parent interference of any sort threatens the order teachers cultivate with such care. As a result, despite shared interest in the welfare of the individual child, teachers often find themselves at odds with parents. Lightfoot (1978, pp. 22–23) sees these conflicts as rooted in the tension between the necessarily collective, universalistic approach teachers must rely on to cope with large groups of children on a daily basis, and the individualized, particularistic lens through which parents see their own child.

Add to this the negative images of poor, minority, and recent immigrant parents that teachers carry with them, and it is no surprise that the "natural enmity" between teachers and parents (McPherson, 1972) should be exacerbated in the case of these poor, minority, and recent immigrant parents. Under these circumstances, as important as teachers believe the "involvement" of parents to be, it is extremely difficult for this to become a reality. This, then, is the picture of the home-school connection painted in the recent research, especially with respect to poor, minority, and immigrant families. What is missing from this portrait, however, is the extent to which the ambiguities of the teacher-parent relationship color teachers' perspectives on the entire enterprise of education. Teachers want parent involvement, but they also intuitively recognize that undertaking parent involvement is full of uncertainty and can also be a risky venture. With the exception of Lightfoot, most research on parent involvement and its consequences fail to recognize the amount of mental and emotional energy teachers invest in evaluating and responding to children's home lives. Again and again, teachers return to the home-school connection, especially in their remarks about children's language abilities, social skills, emotional needs, and learning styles. Furthermore, teachers talk at greater length about their relationships with parents than do anyone else in the school, and not simply because they are the ones most likely to see parents. Thus, although parents do interact with principals, with reading specialists, and occasionally with district officials and school board members, the home-school connection is best understood in the context of the teacher-parent relationship. The preceding findings help to explain some of the puzzles and tensions that characterize teachers' responses to parental involvement in the education of their children.

RESEARCHERS' INSIGHTS ABOUT PARENTS' HOME LITERACY ENVIRONMENTS

While teachers have continued to return to home-school connections, especially in their remarks about children's language abilities, social skills, emotional needs, and learning styles, teachers, at the same time, have consciously and/or unconsciously justified why getting to know the families of the children they teach presents too many difficulties. With work that has been done over the last twenty years, researchers have provided insight into the most significant barriers to effective communication between parents and teachers. From our examination of the literature, four key points emerged about home literacy environments:

1. Teachers do not have access to the "hidden" literacies and "funds of knowledge" in the everyday lives of families and their children, literacy events that might or might not match school expectations (see Anderson and Stokes, 1984; Gonzalez, Moll, Tenery, Rivera, Rendon, Gonzales, and Amanti, 1995; Moll, Amanti, Neff, and Gonzalez, 1992; Moll and Greenberg, 1990; Moll and Diaz, 1987).

Karen walks into her classroom each and every day without knowledge of what occurs in her students' lives outside of school especially around reading and writing. At a staff meeting, Karen's principal suggested that teachers do "home visits." Karen decided to visit the homes of a few of her students, but she is still fuzzy and unclear about what she observed. She shared this with one of her colleagues: "You know when I have made observations in homes that mirror what I expected to see—books, paper, pencils, newspapers—I have a sense of what I am looking at. However, in my visit to the homes of the students who are quite different from me, I might have observed something that was extremely important, but I didn't know what to look for."

Anderson and Stokes (1984) reported that many of the literacy experiences that occur in the homes of poor families were easy to underestimate because as educators we tend to look for activities such as reading storybooks to children and helping children with homework, while overlooking the range of reading and writing experiences that young children in poor families engaged in or observed. However, Anderson and Stokes revealed the sources of experiences in literacy, in addition to typical school or "literacy-for-literacy's sake" activities that poor children did engage in or observed. These included literacy events for daily living needs (e.g., paying bills, obtaining welfare assistance), entertainment (e.g., solving a crossword puzzle, reading a television guide), and religion (e.g., Bible-reading sessions with children).

Building on the work of Anderson and Stokes, Moll and his colleagues noted that, in contrast to classrooms where a student's relationship with a teacher is often one dimensional (that is, we typically interact on a limited number of levels in a limited setting), the family social network is "flexible, adaptive, and active, and may involve multiple persons from outside the homes (Moll, Amanti, Neff, and Gonzalez, 1991, p. 133). Moll *et al.* term this kind of network "thick" and "multi-stranded," and note that "the person from whom the child learns carpentry, for example, may also be the uncle with whom the child's family regularly celebrates birthdays or organizes barbecues, as well as the person with whom the child's father goes fishing on weekends (p. 133). We need to be able to recognize, learn about, and draw on these networks as we teach children. Recognizing and acknowledging these home networks will provide impetus for and foster communication with parents or adults involved at home with the students. This recognition can open up the classroom, make it accessible and relevant for families, and build parents' and communities' trust of teachers and schools.

2. Teachers should be taught to recognize when home and school cultures are not compatible, because some researchers believe that young children, in particular, are best taught to read in situations compatible with home culture (Au and Mason, 1983; Michaels, 1986, 1981; Heath, 1982).

For the last five years, Pam taught in a rural all-white community and she felt that she was an excellent teacher. The parents and students loved her. She rarely had any complaints. Her husband got a promotion and they were relocated to a large urban setting. Pam is a little nervous, but her previous teaching record makes her feel that she can bond with students and their parents. In the urban setting, Pam's students are all nonwhite; in fact, she has very few white students in her classroom. Instead her students represent a variety of ethnic backgrounds. This year "things" are rocky for her. She realizes on some days that she connects with her students and on other days she does not. She is constantly agonizing over what she did "right" or "wrong" on any given day. She is wondering why her relationship with her students and their parents is like riding a roller coaster. She asks, "How can I stop this roller-coaster syndrome feeling?"

Au and Mason (1983), for example, investigated this issue with students of Polynesian-Hawaiian ancestry. Teachers who insisted that Hawaiian children speak one at a time in answering their questions had great difficulty in conducting effective reading lessons. On the other hand, teachers who allowed the children to cooperate or speak together in answering questions could conduct highly effective lessons.

Teachers who used this second style of interaction were teaching in a manner consistent with the rules for *talk story*, an important non-school speech event for Hawaiian children. In talk story, speakers cooperate with one another in telling stories. Rather than one person telling the whole story, two or more speakers take turns, each narrating just a small part. Use of a cooperative talk-story style was important to the students, perhaps because it seems to reflect the value many Hawaiians attach to the performance and wellbeing of the group or family, as opposed to the individual. This example from Au and Mason (1983) illustrates how the effectiveness of reading depends on the teacher taking a broad view of the contexts of literacy and learning to read.

In another example, it was discovered that culturally different children may not be familiar with "sharing time" (or "circle time," "show and tell," etc.) even though it is a common speech event in early elementary school classrooms. Michaels (1986, 1981) reported that when the children's discourse style matched the teacher's own literate style and expectations, collaboration was rhythmically synchronized and allowed for informal practice and instruction in the development of a literate discourse style. For these children, sharing time could be seen as a kind of oral preparation for literacy. In contrast, Michaels noted that when the child's narrative style was in variance with the teacher's expectations, collaboration was often unsuccessful. For example, the teacher would often interrupt students while they were talking rather than guiding or supporting them in making the most out of the event. She concluded that "Sharing time could either provide or deny access to key literacy-related experiences, depending, ironically, on the degree to which teacher and child start out "sharing" a set of discourse conventions and interpretive strategies" (p. 423).

Culturally different children may not be familiar with classroom question-and-answering routines. Evidence for this idea comes from a study by Heath (1982). She compared the use of questions in three settings: Trackton, a working class black community; the classrooms of the children from this community; and the homes of their teachers. In the classrooms and teachers' homes, Heath found that teachers often asked questions for the purpose of "training" children. The children were expected to give answers already known by the adult. When the child was looking at a book, such questions would include: "What's that?" "Where's the puppy?"

In Trackton, on the other hand, children were not generally asked questions for which the adult already knew the answer. Instead, they were asked open-ended questions with answers unknown to the adult. For example, in the passage below, the grandmother's first question has to do with what her grandson is planning to do next with the crayons. Another type of question often asked of Trackton children called for them to make comparisons, stating how one thing was like another. As shown in the passage, the grandmother's second question called the boy's attention to the fact that one of the crayons was the same color as his pants. Heath writes:

> At early ages, Trackton children recognized situations, scenes, personalities, and items, which were similar. However, they never volunteered, nor did adults ask them, to name the attributes, which were similar and added up to one thing's being like another. A grandmother playing with her grandson aged 2 years and 4 months; asked him as he fingered crayons in a box: "Whatcha gonna do with those, huh?" "Ain't dat [color] like your pants?" She then volunteered to me "We don't talk to our chil'un like you folks do; we don't ask 'em' bout colors, names, 'n things." (p. 117)

As the work of Heath suggests, when teachers and children are unable to collaborate or "hook up" in a way that allows teaching to take place, students' learning to read is bound to suffer.

3. Teachers tend to ignore the "cultural variables" (i.e., social organization, sociolinguistics, cognition, and motivation) and potential "cultural conflicts" (i.e., learning style, interactional or relational style, communication, and differing perceptions of involvement) that contribute to the disconnection between home and school literacies (see Tharp, 1989; Gilbert and Gay, 1985).

Connie, like many of us, is not necessarily concerned with the variety of differences found in our classrooms. Yes, Connie is fully aware that children come from different cultures, but that is "something" that she addresses on "culture day." At Connie's school, once a year they encourage parents and students to dress up in costumes, bring food that represents their culture, sing cultural songs, and perform native dances. Connie is not convinced that she should focus on the differences among her students. In fact, she stated "When I have focused on differences in the past in my classroom, it divided my learning community." One class motto that Connie often refers to: "We are more alike than different." What Connie is missing is the point that children might not be more alike than different. However, we must ask ourselves "Are all children's home and school literacies equally valued at school?" In recent years, some of us are beginning to move away from the stance that Connie espouses.

Researchers have identified some "cultural variables" that contribute to this disconnection. These cultural variables may be compatible or incompatible with the expectations and structures of schools. Tharp (1989) has suggested at least four variables: *social organization, sociolinguistics, cognition, and motivation.* Gilbert and Gay (1985) have identified four areas of potential cultural conflict: *learning style, interactional or relational style, communication, and differing perceptions of involvement.* What teachers need to do now is to consider these "cultural variables" in conjunction with the potential areas of conflict. That is, they need to think more about how particular ways of living, communicating, and thinking affect learning, interactions, and perceptions.

Some teachers and a growing number of policy makers impatiently demand, "Tell me about the culture of these kids . . ." (meaning students of color and poor students) or, "Give me some tips that will help me to teach them." These teachers usually want a recipe for teaching students whom they believe to be culturally deprived or culturally different; or they want a list of "do's and don'ts" that will keep "these students" on task.

Similarly, other teachers will say, "I have heard that these kids learn differently because they are 'culturally different' and/or 'linguistically different' and are socialized differently. What does research say about the way these students learn and are socialized? Will this information help me to do a better job teaching them? Where can I get this information?"

Despite the fact that some of us inquire about the cultures of our students, Sonia Nieto (1992) revealed that:

> Many teachers and schools, in an attempt to be color-blind, do not want to acknowledge cultural or racial differences. "I don't see Black or White," a teacher will say. "I see only students." This statement assumes that to be color-blind is to be fair, impartial, and objective. It sounds fair and honest and ethical, but the opposite may actually be true. That is, to see differences, in this line of reasoning, is to see defects and inferiority. Thus, to be color-blind may result in refusing to accept differences and therefore accepting the dominant culture as the norm. It may result in denying the very identity of our students, thereby making them invisible. What seems on the surface to be impeccably fair may in reality be fundamentally unfair. Being color-blind can be positive if it means being non-discriminatory in attitude and behavior. However, it is sometimes used as a way to deny differences that help make us who we are (p. 109).

4. Teachers sometimes "rush to judgment" and hold false assumptions about families and children and are unaware of their own "cultural baggage" (see Paley, 1979; Richardson, Casanova, Placier, and Guilfoyle, 1988; Mills and Buckley, 1992).

Tracy is almost at the point of changing professions. She believes that her teacher education program did not prepare her to work with the kind of students in her classroom. She finds herself constantly blaming her students and their parents. She is frustrated throughout the school year and could have predicted in September when the children entered her classroom who was going to be promoted to the next grade. She says, "I send homework sheets, but the parents don't take the time to help the students complete the work. I don't think my students or their parents care about education— maybe it is not an important part of their culture. I wonder sometimes why am I here?"

Recognizing and accepting the challenge of educating today's students does not guarantee success. Many of us struggle with when to use the training, the knowledge, or tools to work with today's students—especially those students who are classified as at-risk. Vivian Paley (1979), the author of *White Teacher,* took time to reflect on her beliefs and attitudes toward children and how teachers tend to label them. Paley stated:

Each year I greet thirty new children with a clear picture in mind of who shall be called "bright" and who shall be called "well-behaved." Ask me where these " facts" come from and I will probably refer to my professional background. Yet, I doubt that the image I carry of the intelligent, capable child has changed much since my own elementary school days. It has been intellectualized and rationalized . . . (p. 11).

It is no surprise that by the end of the first month of school, most teachers know whom will pass and who will fail. This set of expectations, usually supported by school policies and practices, creates a self-fulfilling prophecy so that the final grading of students is almost exactly what was expected at the outset. Such anticipation exemplifies the kind of mindset which fixes the academic goals of teachers and students, reduces motivation for teaching and learning, and systematically destroys the ego and self-concept of a sizeable group of students often classified as "at-risk."

Frustrated by this reality, Aragon (1977) concluded, "the true impediment to cultural pluralism is that we have had culturally deficient educators attempting to teach culturally different children" (p. 78). This reality also frustrates parents whose children are affected. Oftentimes, parents feel that there

is no use in them becoming involved. Many parents wonder "what difference will it make when 'those teachers' don't understand 'me or my child.'"
However, Anderson (1988) notes that, in some cases, the deficiency can begin
with an educator's understanding of his or her own cultural baggage. All of
us have cultural dimensions to ourselves which include personality, values, social backgrounds, self-concepts, motivations, fears, courage, comfort, personal
deficits, loneliness, and feelings of power or powerlessness (Anderson, 1988).
According to Mills and Buckley (1992), these implicit dimensions, together
with explicit factors such as age, sex, class, race, and physical handicaps, typ-
ify the cultural baggage that educators, as well as students, bring to learning
situations. Essentially, Mills and Buckley contend that "culture is the ultimate
source of the rules by which teachers consciously and unconsciously operate
as they design and deliver instruction, set role expectations for themselves and
students, assign value to students' contributions, and interpret the behavior of
students" (p. 143). The dominance of the "culture" Mills and Buckley speak
of is particularly evident in the interpretation of what is "normal." In other
words, what is normal for us may not be normal for our students or our students' parents. Richardson, Casanova, Placier, and Guilfoyle (1988) studied
how teachers decide who is at risk and how they attribute causes of risk. They
found that:

> The teachers were generally unwilling to attribute a student's lack of success
> to a characteristic inherent in the child or to their own instructional pro-
> grams. They therefore moved outside the classroom to find the cause of the
> student's problems. These causes often rested on their students' home lives
> and parents (p. 37).

The teachers viewed students not at-risk as coming from strong families
and so-called at-risk students as coming from deficient families. Therefore,
"teachers appeared to accept any negative statement about families of at-risk
students from teachers or adults in the building" (Richardson, Casanova, Placier, and Guilfoyle, 1988, p. 37). The term "at-risk" has replaced "culturally
handicapped," "educationally disoriented," "educationally disadvantaged,"
"slum children," "experienced poor," and "unconstitutionally segregated."
Richardson and Colfer (1990) believe that "at-riskness" should not be just another faddish term for troubled students or a descriptor that predicts the like-
lihood of a student's school failure and operates as a mechanism for blaming
the victim. They expressed concern about the popular use of the term in
newspapers, journals, speeches, and "even in the policy literature," which im-
plies that the definition and the condition are absolute. On the contrary, they
say, in school practice the condition is "quite fluid"; a student can be "at-risk"

at one time and not at another, and in one class but not in another. It depends on the "culture" guiding the rules by which our schools operate.

How then do schools and teachers connect home and school literacies to reduce "at-riskness" in various circumstances? Perhaps they can do so by acknowledging and valuing different literacies equally.

A PATH TO FOLLOW: USING PARENT STORIES AS A GUIDE

We asked how teachers could acknowledge and value different literacies equally when no mechanism currently exists for teachers to collect this type of information? We agree with Berger's (1991) observation that "the school must be a support system working cooperatively with the home rather than another agency viewing the parents as failures" (p. 117). Consequently, we believe that parent stories can be the vehicle that will allow teachers to recognize, understand, and respect parents' and children's cultural/social backgrounds.

Over the last five years, it appears that "stories are, at long last, coming into their own as a text—a data base—for researchers" (Jensen, 1989, p. xvi). Vygotsky (1978) has argued for the value of stories noting that:

> Telling stories is . . . a meaning-making process. When people tell stories, they select details of their experience from their stream of consciousness . . . It is this process of selecting constitutive details of experience, reflecting on them, giving them order, and thereby making sense of them that makes telling stories a meaning-making experience . . . Every word that people use in telling their stories is a microcosm of their consciousness (pp. 236–237).

While the value of stories has been documented, it has not been fashionable to value literacy stories from parents of young children as a source of knowledge and wisdom for describing their own home literacy environment. Instead, the research literature is saturated mainly with researchers' descriptions, interpretations, observations, and assumptions of what goes on in the home literacy environments of parents of successful and unsuccessful readers. What is glaringly missing from these researchers' in-depth accounts of what they saw, heard, and recorded in the parents' home literacy environments are the parents' own descriptions and interpretations.

Oftentimes the outsider (e.g., researcher) does not recognize the everyday literacy practices and interactions that are embedded within family cultures as literacy practices. Perhaps one of the overriding reasons researchers are unaware or might not recognize these everyday literacy practices is due to the fact that researchers tend to go into home literacy environments in an a priori fashion. They tend to use "traditional" or preset guidelines/checklists to measure what emergent literacy practices should look like, thus potentially missing the local practices and meanings that are specific to particular families. Some researchers have simply avoided face-to-face contact with parents, especially parents whose children are labeled as "at-risk" of school failure. Instead they have attempted to gather information about students in classrooms via school records and through talking with teachers (Armstrong, 1994). Even though researchers believe that parents are true experts and ought to be enlisted in efforts to identify and share their child's literacy history, little research has investigated home literacy environments from the parents' stance (Anderson and Stokes, 1984). Few studies have been conducted which allow parents to tell their "own stories," and as a result, teachers have not perceived this information as relevant to their literacy teaching practices (Auerbach, 1989; Taylor and Dorsey-Gaines, 1988; Anderson and Stokes, 1984; Snow, 1987; Delgado-Gaitan, 1987).

The time has come for us to allow parents to tell their "own stories." As stated earlier, teachers make presumptions about where their students will be at the end of the year. Many teachers do not themselves have a path to follow that will allow them to reach the goals they have set for their students. Drawing on the recommendations Steven Covey (1989) outlined in his book *Seven Habits of Highly Effective People,* which suggests beginning with the end in mind, teachers will be able to envision where they want to be at the end of the year—in terms of knowing their students and their students' families, and in terms of where they want their students to be in their educational and social growth. We understand, as Vivian Paley does, that impressions are quickly formed at the beginning of the year. We believe that if teachers use the idea of parent stories at the beginning of the year and throughout the year, they will have a path to follow.

REFERENCES

Anderson, J. A. 1988. "Cognitive Styles and Multicultural Populations." *Journal of Teacher Education* 39(1): 2–9.

Anderson, A. B., and S. J. Stokes. 1984. "Social and Institutional Influences on the Development and Practice of Literacy." In *Awakening to Literacy,* ed. H. Goelman, A. Oberg, and F. Smith, 24–37. Exeter, NH: Heinemann.

Aragon, J. 1973. "An Impediment to Cultural Pluralism: Culturally Deficient Educators Attempting to Teach Culturally Different Children." In *Cultural Pluralism in Education: A Mandate for Change,* ed. M. D. Stent, W. R. Hazard, and H. N. Rivlin, 77–84. New York: Appleton-Century-Croft.

Armstrong, T. 1994. *Multiple Intelligences in the Classroom.* Alexandria, VA: Association for Supervision and Curriculum Development.

Au, K. H., and J. M. Mason. 1983. "Cultural Congruence in Classroom Participation Structures: Achieving a Balance of Rights." *Discourse Processes,* **6**(2): 145–167.

Auerbach, E. R. 1989. "Toward a Social-Contextual Approach to Family Literacy." *Harvard Educational Review* 59(2): 165–181.

Berger, E. H. 1991. *Parents as Partners in Education: The School and Home Working Together.* Columbus, OH: Charles E. Merrill.

Carew, J. V., and S. L. Lightfoot. 1979. *Beyond Bias: Perspectives on Classrooms.* Cambridge, MA: Harvard University Press.

Covey, S. 1989. *Seven Habits of Highly Effective People.* New York: Simon & Schuster.

Coleman, J. S., E. Q. Campbell, C. J. Hobson, J. McPartland, A. M. Mood, F. D. Weinfeld, and R. L. Fort. 1966. *Equality of Educational Opportunity.* Washington, DC: U. S. Government Printing Office.

Delgado-Gaitan, C. 1987. "Mexican Adult Literacy: New Directions for Immigrants." In *Becoming Literate in English as a Second Language,* ed. S. R. Goldman and K. Trueba, 9–32. Norwood, NJ: Ablex.

Fullan, M. 1982. *The Meaning of Educational Change.* New York: Teachers College Press.

Gilbert, S. E., and G. Gay. 1985. "Improving the Success in School of Poor Black Children." *Phi Delta Kappan,* **67**(2): 133–137.

Garcia, E. 1994. *Understanding and Meeting the Challenge of Student Cultural Diversity.* Boston: Houghton Mifflin Company.

Gonzalez, N., L. C. Moll, M. F. Tenery, A. Rivera, P. Rendon, R. Gonzales, and C. Amanti. 1995. "Funds of Knowledge for Teaching in Latino Households." *Urban Education* 29(4): 443–470.

Heath, S. B. 1982. "What no Bedtime Story Means: Narrative Skills at Home and School." *Language in Society* 11(2): 49–76.

Jensen, J. M. 1989. "Introduction." In *Stories to Grow On: Demonstrations of Language Learning in K–8 Classrooms,* ed. J. M. Jensen, XV–XX. Portsmouth, NH: Heinemann.

Lightfoot, S. L. 1978. *Worlds Apart: Relationships between Families and Schools.* New York: Basic Books.

Lortie, D. C. 1975. *Schoolteacher: A Sociological Study.* Chicago: University of Chicago Press.

McPherson, G. H. 1972. *Small Town Teacher.* Cambridge, MA: Harvard University Press.

Michaels, S. 1986. "Narrative presentation: An Oral Preparation for Literacy with First Graders." In *The Social Construction of Literacy,* ed. J. Cook-Gumperz, 94–116. New York: Cambridge University Press.

Michaels, S. 1981. "Sharing Time": Children's Narrative Styles and Differential Access to Literacy." *Language in Society* 10: 423–442.

Mills, J. R., and C. W. Buckley. 1992. "Accommodating the Minority Teacher Candidate: Non-Black Students in Predominately Black Colleges." In *Diversity in Teacher Education: New Expectations,* ed. M. E. Dilworth, 134–159. San Francisco: Jossey-Bass Publishers.

Moll, L. C., C. Amanti, D. Neff, and N. Gonzalez. 1992. "Funds of Knowledge for Teaching: Using a Qualitative Approach to Connect Homes and Classrooms." *Theory Into Practice* XXXI (2): 132–141.

Nieto, S. 1992. *Affirming Diversity: The Sociopolitical Context of Multicultural Education.* New York: Longman.

Paley, V. G. 1979. *White Teacher.* Cambridge, MA: Harvard University Press.

Richardson, V., and P. Colfer. 1990 . "Being At-Risk in School." In *Access to Knowledge: An Agenda for Our Nation's Schools,* ed. J. I. Goodlad and P. Keating, 107–124. New York: College Entrance Examination Board.

Richardson-Koehler, V., U. Casanova, P. Placier, K. Guilfoyle. 1988. *School Children At-Risk.* London: Falmer.

Snow, C. 1987. "Factors Influencing Vocabulary and Reading Achievement in Low Income Children." In *Toegepaste Taalwentenschap in Artikelen,* ed. R. Apple. Special 2,124–128. Amsterdam: ANELA.

Swap, S. M. 1993. *Developing Home-School Partnerships: From Concepts to Practice.* New York: Teachers College.

Swap, S. M. 1992. "Parent Involvement and Success for All Children: What We Know Now." In *Home-School Collaboration: Enhancing Children's Academic and Social Competence,* ed. A. L. Christenson and J. C. Conoley, 53–80. Silver Springs, MD: The National Association of School Psychologists.

Taylor, D., and C. Dorsey-Gaines. 1988. *Growing Up Literate: Learning from Inner-City Families.* Portsmouth, NH: Heinemann.

Tharp, R. G. 1989. "Psychocultural Variables and Constants: Effects on Teaching and Learning in Schools." *American Psychologist* 44(2): 349–359.

Vygotsky, L. S. 1978. *Mind in Society.* Cambridge, MA: Harvard University Press.

2

At-Risk Students
and Parental Involvement

We can't all and some of us don't. That's all there is to it.

—Eeyore in *Winnie-the-Pooh*, A. A. Milne

THE BOTTOM LINE

In the last chapter we discussed the research on parent involvement and some important ideas that have defined how we think about this subject. We also gave you information about research on the communication between home and school and between parents and teachers. The bottom line is that nearly everyone agrees that parent involvement is important and that teachers and parents should communicate with each other as often as possible so that children's learning and development can be supported inside and outside of school. Still, there's another bottom line that many of us are all too familiar with—the fact that having productive conversations with parents is difficult and sometimes practically impossible. Even though we know this is true, how well do we understand the factors that combine to make many of our interactions and conversations with parents difficult? This chapter is devoted to answering the question of what makes productive and positive communication between teachers and parents easy to verbally support, but very hard to do.

TIME AND OPPORTUNITY

We often begin our teaching careers with grand plans and ideas designed to educate our students, promote our own learning and development, and involve the community in what happens in our classroom. We recognize that parent involvement is an extremely important factor in the success of our students, and we start out by attempting to do everything we can to help parents understand what's going on in our classrooms, and what they can do to support their child's learning. However, it doesn't take long before we understand that our time is very limited, and we quickly learn that choices have to be made and priorities established. Should I devote extra time and energy to my reading program? Or should I direct my efforts toward developing a workshop on how parents can read to their children? Should I spend the little time I have outside the classroom on issues of the social development of my three most difficult students? Or should I perhaps try to create parent volunteer modules so that parents feel more welcome and useful when they visit my classroom? It would be wonderful if we could say "yes" to all the things that we would like to do, but the truth is that sometimes certain things seem more important than others do. And it's not as if we aren't ever going to do things to help parents connect with us and with their child . . . those things just go on the back burner while we tend to some of the more critical issues of teaching and learning.

In addition to the limitations of time, we are also limited by our opportunities. Unless we are lucky enough to work in a school in which parents and teachers have "built-in" daily interaction with each other, it is extremely difficult to know when and where the best opportunities exist to encourage the parents of our students to become more involved in their child's education. For the majority of us, the opportunities to interact with parents come at very specific points during the school year: At the beginning when we greet students and parents, at parent-teacher conferences, and perhaps at the end of the year. The fact of the matter is that these times are markers for us. Although we think about students' progress all the time, we gauge our success with students by where they are at the beginning, in the middle, and at the end of the school year. The time between these markers can seem so short that it appears impossible to fill part of it with attempts to make more opportunities to talk with parents.

And yet, we know that it is necessary. We know from the research, and we know in our hearts, that we have to try to help parents understand how important it is that they work with their children and have a good line of communication with the school. And so, even though our time and opportunity is severely constrained, we continue to try strategy after strategy to involve parents in what goes on at school and to learn more about what goes on in students' homes.

EXPECTATIONS

Another clue to understanding why parents and teachers have difficulty connecting with one another lies in the expectations that each brings to understanding what children are supposed to learn and do in school, and how they are to contribute to the children's progress. Let's face it: As human beings, we all have expectations that guide our understanding of how we should deal with the myriad of different things that happen in our daily lives. Parents and teachers are no different from everyone else. They often have specific expectations about what is supposed to happen in school and what they are supposed to do to support children's learning. However, problems arise when teachers and parents have expectations of each other that differ. To prove this, think for a moment about a parent you've known in the past who seemed to agree with your teaching philosophy and with your ideas about how they should be involved in their child's education (and actually followed through with what you suggested). Your communication with this parent probably seemed effortless. In fact, maybe you'd found yourself wishing that all of the parents you encountered were her, but realized that many of the parents you talked with were not.

These differing expectations have several sources. In Chapter One, we discussed Lightfoot's (1978) research, which outlined how parents and teachers have different ideas because the roles they occupy are different—parents deal with one child, teachers deal with a large group of children. More specifically, it is often difficult for parents to perceive the difficulties that their child has when the only other children they have for comparison are their other children or their neighbor's children! When we are in our classrooms, we have many other children to use as comparisons for what is appropriate learning and behavior (in addition to what we learned in our preparation for teaching). As teachers, we often see our students in shades of gray—we notice the subtle variations, issues, strengths, and weaknesses in our students' abilities. On the other hand, parents seem to see their children in black and white—either they do know their colors, know how to spell, know how to do long division, or they don't.

Differing expectations may also create problems when parents and teachers communicate if parents see themselves as complete authorities on what is best for their children, or when parents think of teachers as holding all of the answers or solutions:

Beth and Megan are two teachers who are friends and who work in the same school teaching language arts to different groups of fourth graders. After the first night of parent-teacher conferences, Beth rushes over to Megan's classroom to talk with her about Mrs. Metcalf, the mother of Kevin. "You know Megan, even though I know that Mrs. Metcalf is a school counselor, she just came to her conference and . . . it was like she had suddenly lost all of her training and professional knowledge and looked to me as the one who could solve all of Kevin's behavior problems! I can even tell you how frustrating it is to want to work with her but to have her 'play dead' when I ask her to help me find solutions!" With an exhausted smile Megan replies "Well, I don't know what's worse, having a parent with expertise 'play dead,' or having a parent who obviously has never had experience teaching but thinks they wrote the book on what a fourth grader needs to know about poetry. I just got done trying to talk with Mr. Perkins, and I just know he left here thinking that I know absolutely nothing about how to prepare his daughter for next year. I've gotten to the point where I'm not going to waste my time trying to convince him that all of my years of training and teaching really do make a difference in what I know."

As we think about Beth and Megan's situations, it becomes clear that it's hard to know how to approach parents without creating the perception that they are making a judgment about the parent themselves. How do you tell a parent that they might have good ideas, but that you are the one who has to make the final decision about a child's reading group level? How do you re-assure a parent and ask for their help without having them think that you don't know what to do about a child's attention problems? There are no easy answers to these types of questions, but they are examples of problems related to expectations that teachers have to deal with every day.

PROBLEM SITUATIONS MAKE DIFFICULT CONVERSATIONS

We all realize that talking to the parents of children who are doing well is usually easier than talking to the parents of children who are not. Often, what makes these conversations especially difficult is the fact that "the apple doesn't fall far from the tree." Parents often have characteristics that are similar to that of their children. For example, if a child is having difficulty learning to read, a parent may simply dismiss this, saying, "well, when I was his age I had trouble learning to read, too." Or, if a child is having trouble sitting down in class and staying on task without bothering other children, a parent may see this as normal behavior, because they themselves have trouble maintaining their attention for longer than a few minutes.

Unfortunately, the conversations we need to have with parents are often focused around problems that their children are having in the classroom. What often results is a lose-lose situation. Parents are either put on the defensive and feel that teachers are criticizing them, or they are forced into complacency, and feel as if they have no choice but to go with what the teacher and other school professionals are saying. As the bearer of bad news (your child is flunking math, your child has not learned letter-to-sound correspondence, your child got into her third fight this week) we are left feeling like the "bad guy." No one wins in these kinds of situations because a good rapport with parents rarely gets established. This realization often leads us right back to where we began—as teachers we wish we had the time and opportunity (and skills!) to establish a rapport with parents that would allow us to more effectively communicate with each other for the benefit of children.

Even if we acknowledge all of the difficulties of establishing positive communication with parents, we are left with the fact that regardless of who or where we teach, we will encounter students who can be considered "at-risk" in one way or another, or children who could be doing better, even though they're considered "normal." As we think about how to establish better communication with parents, our reflection begins with the students we work with in our classrooms. Below are some examples of students that a group of teachers considered at-risk. As you read their descriptions, take note of the similarities some of these children might bear to the children in your classroom—and think about how difficult it would be to have meaningful and productive conversations about these students with their parents.

SOUND FAMILIAR?

Juan

Juan is in the fourth grade and he's about four feet and six inches tall with a stocky build. He is Hispanic, with black hair and dark brown eyes. His posture is bent over and many times he comes into the classroom smelling like human feces. Juan is not very motivated and does not work hard. In group situations he will talk, and he's not a loner. He will sometimes work, depending on his partner. He seems sad most of the time in work situations. Kevin is the person he hangs around with the most. Juan loves low riders, and writing has been his most successful subject so far. When Juan works one on one, he still has a hard time staying on task, unless it is with myself or the student teacher. He is behind academically and is just beginning to understand place value. Juan trusts me with information about his family and feels free to share background information with me.

Brad

Brad is five years old and is very overweight. His face is red most of the time. He is pleasant most of the time, but when something doesn't go his way he lays down on the floor, face down, and cries very loud. When someone looks at him, he yells "don't even think about staring at me!" If something catches his interest he stops crying and it's as if he never had a problem at all. He has a difficult time sitting in a group; he rolls on the floor, talks to others, and touches other children. Brad loves to construct things with Lego's, blocks, etc. He loves outdoor activities, but sometimes he gets so red and out of breath that it concerns me. (The bottom line is) as long as he is getting what he wants, he's happy.

Beth

Beth is small for her age, is often ill, extremely shy, and eleven years old. Beth is unaware of the fact that she is behind other students and is cooperative and very motivated, but often frustrated by school. She usually works alone and works very hard, does what she is asked, follows directions, turns in work without having to be told, but has great difficulty. Beth interacts with others, but does not speak in class, does not take risks, will not give opinions, and follows our class discussions but does not participate. She interacts with me, wants to do well, wants to please me, but is nervous and shy.

Renae

Renae is a fourth grader who comes to the resource room for reading assistance. She is of medium build; slightly stocky with brown eyes and thin light brown hair that has been cut very short on the crown. Renae is very talkative and open in her conversation and is very willing to come to the resource room, but will often try to sidetrack the tasks she is supposed to do with other "fun" ideas and is very distracted by other students. Renae has difficulty with multi-step processes, is a very poor reader, has poor eye-hand coordination and seems to have problems with remembering from day to day what she has worked very hard to figure out the day before, especially when it comes to new words. She seems to have a lot on her mind that she needs to get around before she can focus on the task. Mathematics, even on the computer, seems to intimidate her, as does opening a book. Renae is very social and makes a point of introducing me as her best friend.

David

David is an active and energetic five-year-old boy in my classroom. He is very social and constantly craves attention. He is one of my brightest students, and is always ready to learn more academically. However, his social skills leave much to be desired. During group work he constantly tries to take over by participating out of turn and by telling others what to do, and this results in a time out for him or not participating in the activity. His parents do not take preventative measures to correct and alter his behavior, despite several conferences. Further, they encourage his behavior by ignoring it.

Kelly

Kelly is a five-year-old girl who rides the bus and comes in each day looking on the "unkempt" side. Kelly often has a runny nose, dirty hands and fingernails, and her hair is long and often not combed. Kelly's clothes are always wrinkled and well worn and she has tennis shoes she wears every day with long laces that are constantly untied! Kelly does not know how to tie yet, so I tie them many times a day. Kelly is generally quiet on the surface, but is fidgety and often whispering to others when the attention is not directly on her. She seems to try and be "sneaky" about talking to others, bouncing in the hallway instead of walking and being silly in a way that is not overtly noticeable but always under the surface. Sometimes when I look at Kelly there is a gleam in her eyes and I just know she is up to something! She is not a behavior problem, but she is also hard to capture in terms of seeing her very involved or interested in what we are doing. Kelly is average in terms of skill level at this time, but I see her as a child who will be easily "missed" by teachers because she is quiet on the surface, but her mind is always turning. Kelly is very loving and eats up all the attention she is given.

Whether we have opportunities to talk about it or not, we all know that it is not easy to work with the children such as those described above. Often it is hard to know where to begin, especially when the nature of a child's "at-riskness" is difficult to address and is not easily put into words. Added to this are the multiple ways that educators and other professionals define "at-risk." Depending on your place in the educational system, and on what student population you work with, you may define at-risk in one or more of the following ways:

- may not attain reading and writing skills high enough to go on to next grade
- has been/is physically, sexually, or mentally abused
- is malnourished or sleep deprived
- is part of a one-parent household
- lacks adequate communication skills
- does not have appropriate social behavior with other students and the teacher
- cannot maintain attention needed to complete classroom tasks and activities
- is physically or mentally challenged

In an effort to pinpoint the origin of a child's difficulty, many of us intuitively direct our attention to the home life of students. This attention is not misdirected; as indicated in the previous chapter, many of the problems children face in school occur as the result of dissonance between their home and school lives. However, when we direct our attention to the home lives of students, we also carry preformed ideas about those students. We may draw on information we have learned about parents through our interactions with them and through talking to other teachers.

Given this fact and the difficulties of parent-teacher communication that have been discussed in this chapter, there are some important questions that need to be asked and answered before we can do a better job of educating all of our students. How do we learn more about students considered at-risk? How do we learn about the home lives and parents of these students? How can we overcome barriers imposed by little time and opportunity and by our differing expectations and beliefs in order to establish productive relationships with parents? The answers to these questions are important if we are to lay a strong foundation for understanding the students we teach that is based on more than casual conversations and mental notations. One source for answers are parent stories. In the next chapter we discuss the questions that we may need to ask parents in order to gain the crucial information that can make a difference between success or failure for children in our classrooms.

A FINAL, VERY IMPORTANT THOUGHT

In reading this chapter, chances are that you've probably agreed with the idea that time, opportunity, differing expectations (on the part of parents and teachers), problem situations, and at-risk children all make communication between parents and teachers extremely difficult. However, what you must emphasize to yourself is that these are obstacles—and as obstacles, they *can* be overcome. Having productive and constructive conversations with parents is not easy—but it can be done.

As in anything, you must prepare mentally before you can be successful in your actions. In order to mentally prepare yourself to have good communication and productive conversations with students' parents, you must first believe that these kinds of conversations are possible. If you are currently telling yourself that you just can't "reach" a particular parent, chances are that you won't! As a wise person once said, "Whether you believe you can or you can't do a thing, you're right."

Secondly, you must mentally prepare yourself by acknowledging your fears and hesitations about talking with parents. Write down all of these fears and hesitations and ways in which you feel you might not be successful and look at what you've written. There is power in making these things visible because once you can identify obstacles to your goals, you can identify ways to take these obstacles out of your way.

The last step in mentally preparing yourself for productive conversations with parents is to recognize your fears—but to continue on *despite these fears*. That is what being a courageous and caring educator is all about. It is about knowing that you may face challenges and that you may make yourself vulnerable, but that you are still willing to "put yourself out there" if it may bring benefits to the children that you teach. With this in mind, let's move on to the next chapter, "Collecting Parent Stories."

3

Collecting Parent Stories

Children are who they are. They know what they know. They bring what they bring. Our job is not to wish that students knew more or knew differently. Our job is to turn each student's knowledge and diversity of knowledge we encounter into a curricular strength rather than an instructional inconvenience. We can do that only if we hold high expectations for all students, convey great respect for the knowledge and culture they bring to the classroom, and offer lots of support in helping them achieve those expectations.

—P. David Pearson, *"Reclaiming the Center"*

CONTINUING TO BUILD OUR CASE FOR COLLECTING PARENT STORIES

There was a psychiatrist who always asked his patients, "What seems to be the problem?" However, after several years of trying to help his patients improve their health, he began to realize that when he asked this question, his patients gave answers which they thought the doctor wanted to hear. His patients often told him of their symptoms, but many times these descriptions did not get to the root of the problem. Finally, one day while talking to a patient, he asked the patient to start at the beginning by telling him a few stories about her life. This suggestion brought forth a wealth of valuable information, which revealed many things about the patient's present condition. With time, the doctor was able to make sense of the story and effectively help his patients recognize their strengths and overcome their difficulties.

In this story, the doctor realized that a one-word diagnosis was most important to his patients; thus they gave information which they thought would help the doctor make a quick evaluation. However, the doctor understood that paying too much attention to the diagnosis alone could do a lot of harm.

25

Like the doctor's patient in the story, parents of school-age children can fall into the habit of searching for a one-word diagnosis of their child in the form of grades on report cards or achievement test scores. Teachers can also get trapped into thinking of children in terms of their grade performance, or in terms of the kind and quantity of children's home literacy experiences. Many teachers are guilty of asking parents a series of questions about their home literacy practices and environment, which oftentimes require simplistic answers. For example, the questions that they asked have included:

- How many hours per week do you routinely spend reading stories to your child?
- Have you set aside a certain time every day to read to your child?
- Do you encourage your child to read or tell you a story?
- Do you encourage your child to talk and ask questions?
- Do you ask "how," "why," and "when" questions about the stories?
- Do you provide books and magazines for your child to read?
- Do you read to your child, the newspaper, comic books, library books, magazines, or a book of his/her choice?
- Do you encourage your child to use paper and pencil? Have you built a reading atmosphere at home (place, time, library area)?
- Do you talk and listen to your child? Have you provided your child contact with paper and pencil?
- When working in the house or yard, do you talk to your children about what you are doing and why?
- Are your children included in all normal conversation periods such as at dinner or while watching television?
- Do you try to answer questions as completely as you possibly can? If you do not know the answer to your child's question, do you hunt to find a source with the answer?
- Do you give your child simple directions and see if he/she understands and follows them?
- Do you and your child visit the library regularly?
- Do you help your child to select books?
- Do you control your child by setting aside a certain hour every day that your child can watch television?
- Are you selective in the TV programs your child can watch?
- Do you talk about and discuss the program with your child?

A FRAMEWORK FOR ASKING
BETTER QUESTIONS

When teachers ask these types of questions, many parents often answer with one-word responses. Also, many parents tend to provide answers they think teachers would like to hear. Unfortunately, even though we might receive some information about the home literacy environment, many of our "real" questions remain unanswered. However, there is a reason why we continue to ask parents questions like the ones previously listed. Leichter (1984) points out that

> Research efforts to understand the family's contribution to the education of its members, as well as intervention efforts designed to assist families in improving their educational effectiveness, often rest on the assumption that education within families can best be understood and evaluated in terms of models derived from schooling, or even in terms of narrowly conceived outcome measures of school achievement (p. 38).

In other words, the traditional literacy questions that we ask parents concerning reading and writing often originate and center on the context of the school, rather than seeking to integrate the context of the home. What this may mean for teachers and parents is that only one dimension of information about a child's literacy development is discussed. This one dimension, while encompassing some of the important artifacts and activities needed as a foundation for literacy development, does not get at the physical environment, interpersonal interactions, and the emotional and motivational climates which are often just as critical in the development of a child's literacy. Unless all of these dimensions are fully uncloseted, a complete picture of the home literacy environment cannot be revealed. Leichter (1984) argues that

> To describe visual forms in the home, observation must go beyond narrowly defined literacy resources such as print to include a broad range of forms; to locate literacy in the stream of family activities, a broad range of activities carried out for a variety of purposes must be observed, not merely those explicitly done for the purposes of literacy acquisition, and to uncover emotional and motivational climates, data are needed on a range of family motivations and emotions, from the embarrassing and traumatic to the playful and amusing. To obtain a variety of data, a number of data-gathering and data-recording procedures are required, including photographing physical arrangements, videotaping nonverbal interactions, and _tape-recording personal history interviews_ (p. 47).

Leichter (1984) contends that conceptions about the ways in which family environments condition the child's experience with literacy can be clustered into three broad categories, as follows:

- Physical environment: the level of economic and educational resources, the types of visual stimulation, and the physical arrangements of the family set the stage for the child's experiences with literacy.

- Interpersonal Interaction: The child's literacy opportunities are conditioned by moment-to-moment interpersonal interaction with parents, siblings, and other in the household with respect to informal corrections, explanations, and other feedback for the child's experiments with literacy.

- Emotional and motivational climates: The emotional relationships within the home, parental recollections of their experiences with literacy, and the aspirations of family members condition the child's experiences with literacy (p. 40).

We feel that it is important to have parents tell us about their home literacy environment by using Leichter's categories as a framework. Just as the psychiatrist was able to better understand his patient through the use of stories, so might the teacher be able to better understand the student through the storytelling of parents.

GETTING STARTED

Now that you've had a chance to read about the thinking behind parent stories, it's time to start collecting your own parent stories. The first decision you should make is how many you'd like to collect. Although you can collect as many as you'd like, we suggest that you start off with a few, maybe even just one. This way, you can take your time and familiarize yourself with the process. To help you figure out which parents you might like to talk with, we've included some exercises for you to do and think about in the "Getting Focused" section below. However, before deciding which parents you'd like to talk with, you should:

1. Share with your principal/colleagues your plan to collect parent stories and seek their support and encouragement.

You can use the ideas in the introduction to our book to help you build the case for collecting parent stories. In particular, you can stress that parental involvement is acknowledged in vision and mission statements of schools and school charters (McGilp and Michael, 1994). We are confident that you will get a lot of agreement from your principal and colleagues. Also, you can sell the idea of collecting parent stories by pointing out that it is a common practice in other professions like medicine, law, and architecture to collect information as a way of developing a professional interaction with their patients/clients. Then, say to your principal and colleagues that collecting parent stories can become a common practice for establishing a working relationship with families and children.

2. Try to find at least one friend or colleague also willing to collect parent stories.

It's possible to collect parent stories on your own and learn a lot from them. But often we, as teachers, can work best if we have a partner to cajole, nag, support, and encourage us when we need it. The colleague needn't be in the same school or even the same town, but you will need some support to make changes in your teaching and relationship with families and children.

Set aside one hour per week to meet or talk on the phone about the collection of parent stories. It's helpful to list the actual times these conferences will occur for the first three weeks you are working together. Whether it's one person or a dozen, support helps if you are going to make substantial changes in your teaching and relationship with families and children.

GETTING FOCUSED

Make a List of All the Records You Keep
Now Related to Families and Children

You are adding to the body of knowledge that you currently have about your students by collecting parent stories. With this in mind, it is important that you first have a firm understanding of all the ways you already gather information about students. We suggest that you make a list of all the different records that you keep relating to your students. See Figure 3.1, which shows a chart you can use. As you list the records, make sure that you include all of the ways that you keep track of what your students are doing, from the most formal, to the most informal. Additionally, you may also want to specify on the following chart model if you keep certain types of records for some of your students and not others. We encourage you to use your latitude to modify and adapt this form to meet your individual needs.

As you list the records that you keep, think about why you keep them. Ask yourself how often you take them, how often you refer back to them, and what they are for. Could some of the records you keep be eliminated? Before continuing on to the next step involved in getting ready to collect parent stories, you may want to get a handle on the records you already keep. If the

Record What list of student records do I keep?   What purpose(s) do they serve?   Which ones can I eliminate? How frequently do I keep them? (daily, weekly, sporadically)
1.
2.
3.
4.
5.
6.
7.
8.
9.
10.
11.
12.
13.
14.
15.

Figure 3.1 Record Worksheet

records you take now seem random and unfocused, you may want to set a goal of getting more organized—weeding out the kinds of records that don't serve you and your children and families well.

After you finish listing the records that you keep, take just a few minutes to prioritize your goals for collecting parent stories. We know that you may not have the time to ask *all* of the questions on the questionnaire in *one setting*. Further, you may only find it necessary to ask some of the questions included in our questionnaire. We suggest that our questions could serve as a *time release survey* that you could use throughout the school year to uncover what you need to know about families and children. In other words, you may want to choose some specific questions to start out with, and then, after you've been able to talk with a parent, you may want to ask additional questions from the questionnaire, or questions of your own.

Tools of the Trade

Sometimes nothing makes you feel more like a professional than having the right tools. Teachers collecting parent stories need tools. You certainly don't need many—some people would argue that the pad of paper on your desk and the pen in your hand is enough. But we feel that you need some additional equipment. Having a variety of materials at your disposal will enable you to try a variety of strategies for collecting parent stories. There isn't one right way to collect parent stories. Testing out a variety of materials can help you find the right way for you. You'll probably want to schedule some time alone or with your colleague to discuss the possible materials needed for collecting parent stories. Some of these may already be available at your school, or you might want to add them to your supply requests at the start of the school year.

Writing Instruments and a Notebook. Pens, pencils, a notebook: These are simple supplies, but they're still the most useful, especially if you're planning to keep all of your notes and ideas about the parent stories you collect in one place.

Tape Recorder. This is a necessity! By listening to the tape of your conversation with parents, you'll be able to reflect on the important aspects of the conversation. You'll also be able to use the tape in order to make the detailed notes that are a part of collecting parent stories.

Laptop Computer. Great for collecting parent stories and it gives you a leg up on thinking about the parent stories because you already have the information in the computer.

Transcribing Machine. If you plan on tape recording and then transcribing the parent stories, transcribing machines can cut your transcription time by 50 percent. These are modified tape recorders that allow you to vary the speed of the tape through foot pedals and then automatically back up the tape a bit every time you stop the tape while transcribing. Many teachers who do regular interviews with students wonder how they survived without these machines once they try them out.

Photocopy Paper. Many parents do not mind completing questionnaires. You could send home a few questions for parents to complete at selected times throughout the school year.

CHOOSING WHO TO TALK TO

As you go through the process of deciding who to talk to, make sure you consciously try to identify the "prefab" judgments that you have about students and their families. By prefab judgments, we mean those insights you may have about families and children that are based not upon what you're seeing but upon your preconceptions of what your classroom is like and how learning occurs in it. The more specific and concrete you can be about the "cultural variables" that contribute to your being compatible or incompatible with families and children (i.e., social organization, sociolinguistics, cognition, and motivation), the more you will learn from asking the questions on the interview questionnaire. Also, we suggest that you need to think about these "cultural variables" in conjunction with potential areas of conflict (i.e., learning style, interactional or relational style, communication, and differing perceptions of involvement).

As the first step toward getting ready to use the questions we've included at the end of the chapter, we suggest that you list all of the students in your classroom—you can use the chart shown in Figure 3.2. Then, in the next column of the chart, jot down a couple of words that describes each student, academically and/or socially. Our reason for this suggestion is that it allows you to begin thinking about the students you may have questions about. Filling in the chart also helps you to identify information regarding the cultural variables and potential areas of conflict that may come into play as you teach and communicate with students. The questions we have included on the interview questionnaire are organized around the "cultural variables" in conjunction with the potential areas of conflict.

Name of Student	A few of the words I would use to describe this student are....

Figure 3.2 List of Students in Classroom

Choosing Who to Talk To: An Exercise

By beginning to identify which students you might have concerns or questions about, you also have begun to understand which parents you'd like to collect parent stories from. In order to help you get even more specific about your reasons for wanting to gain more information about particular parents' home lives and literacy practices, we've created a set of questions that you can ask yourself.

Questions You Can Ask Yourself

1. In as much detail as possible, describe why you want to talk to _____'s parent(s).

2. If you feel that _____ is a child, who is "at-risk," describe the nature of his/her "at-riskness" in as much detail as possible.

3. In general, what would you like to see happen in order for the student to improve their academic and/or social development?

4. Specifically, what would you like to see happen in order for the student to improve their academic and/or social development?

5. Take a moment to think about your knowledge of this student's parent(s) or caregiver(s). What have others said about them? In what circumstances have you interacted with them? Describe your interactions with them and discuss your intuitive impressions and things they've said that really "stick out" in your mind.

6. Given what you know about your students' parents/caregivers, how easy or difficult do you think it would be to approach them and ask them questions regarding their child's home life and literacy experiences? Why?

7. Do you think you would get the whole story from them? Why or why not?

8. Be creative! Think about three ways you could engage and communicate with this child's parents/caregivers in order to find answers to your questions. Would you offer anything in result for this information? (A personal revelation of your own, a fun instructional book for their child, some suggestions for what they could do at home) If yes, what would you offer? If not, why not?

In order to give you an idea about how other teachers have answered these questions, we've included an example of how one teacher filled out the questions, and we've also given you an opportunity to fill out the questions by thinking of a student and parent who you'd like to talk to.

An Example from Lisa: Her Answers
and Ideas about Who She'd Like to Talk To

1. *If you feel that (_____) is a child who is "at-risk," describe the nature of his/her "at-riskness" in as much detail as possible.*

Erica is a cute, petite blond with glasses. She appears fragile and helpless, and daydreams frequently. She feels that if anything happens, it is not her doing. She places blame on others, and never herself. She can outwait well—if a question is asked and she doesn't want to answer, she can wait forever.

She comes from a family where they verbalize that education is important, but mom is not quite sure how to help her and dad is too busy. She stays quiet and doesn't ask questions. She is also young for the fourth grade, so she is immature too. She appears fragile, so people want to do things for her.

2. *In general, what would you like to see happen in order for the student to improve their academic and/or social development?*

I'd like for her to feel the consequences of not completing assignments, to take responsibility for her actions, for her parents to give her more responsibility at home, and for her to focus, not day dream, and develop the courage to answer and ask questions.

3. *Specifically, what would you like to see happen in order for the student to improve their academic and/or social development?*

I'd like to see her write down her assignments and grade her attentiveness everyday at school. Then I could check this over and she could take it home. Her parents would need to help her with her homework, sign a sheet, and return in the next day.

I would also like to see Erica organize her desk and keep track of her homework better. If she forgets to do something, she'd have to have some kind of consequence—one that she'd decide on. I think it would need to hurt a little for it to be successful.

4. *Take a moment to think about your knowledge of this student's parent(s) or caregiver(s). What have others said about them? In what circumstances have you interacted with them? Describe your interactions with them and discuss your intuitive impressions and things they've said that really "stick out" in your mind.*

Erica's parents are very different from each other. The father is a no-nonsense man who works a lot. The mom is very concerned with appearance and not so much with education. My first impression was "flighty" for the mom and "no-nonsense" for the dad. Dad was very upset with her progress but mom did not seem to get it.

5. *Given what you know about your students' parents/caregivers, how easy or difficult do you think it would be to approach them and ask them questions regarding their child's home life and literacy experiences? Why?*

The mom would be very easy to approach, but I don't think she "gets it"— I can talk to her, but nothing gets done. Dad is more intimidating and demanding, but I get results.

6. *Do you think you would get the whole story from them? Why or why not?*

Not really, because they insist that they are working with her every night for two to three hours. I would really like to find out what it means when they say they are "working with her."

7. *Be creative! Think about three ways you could engage and communicate with this child's parents/caregivers in order to find answers to your questions. Would you offer anything in result for this information? (A personal revelation of your own, a fun instructional book for their child, some suggestions for what they could do at home) If yes, what would you offer? If not, why not?*

I could do a home visit to actually see the home environment. I could also ask to meet them at McDonald's, and maybe talk over dinner. Over the course of the year, maybe I could organize a few potlucks with different groups of parents, and we could talk about what's going on at the school (I could approach them during or after the dinner about Erica). I think before I talk with them, it would be good for me to ask them to come in and sit in on the classroom a couple of times, even if it's only for an hour. Then we could use their observations as a beginning point for our conversations. I also think it might be helpful for me to suggest some kind of activity that brings the home and school together that would help Erica to be more responsible for her actions.

Writing Down Your Own Answers to these Questions

Now that you've had an opportunity to read the preceding example, take some time to answer the seven questions and write down these answers in the space below or in your notebook.

YOU'RE ALMOST READY . . .

By this point, you've identified which parents you'd like to talk to and why, you've probably thought of some places or opportunities in which you could speak to them. The only thing left to do is actually have the conversation. However, before you do, we strongly suggest that you plan to tape record the conversation. Additionally, it is very important for you to take notes about your conversation. These notes can be your general impressions of the conversation, what you think you learned, important ideas that you or the parent brought up, and anything else you think is important to remember. These notes will form the foundational information to be used in the next chapter, which deals with how to make sense of the information you've collected.

DESCRIPTION OF THE EDWARDS–PLEASANTS PARENT STORIES QUESTIONNAIRE

There are fifty (50) questions and eleven categories in this questionnaire. The categories of questions include: (1) parent/child family routines and activities, (2) child's literacy history, (3) teachable moments, (4) homelife, (5) educational experiences, (6) parent's beliefs about their child, (7) child's time with others, (8) parent/child/sibling relationships, (9) parent's hobbies, activities, and interests in books, (10) parent/teacher relationship, and (11) parent's school history—ideas about school.

Parent/Child Family Routines and Activities

1. How did you structure your child's day as s/he was growing up? What routines were followed (conversations or talk time, television programs, bedtime, eating, exercise, etc.)?
2. What is a normal weekday routine for you and your child? What is a normal weekend like?
3. What do you and your child enjoy doing together?
4. What does your family enjoy doing together?

Child Literacy History

5. Tell me about your child at age 1, 2, 3, 4, etc. What interesting things did he/she do at these ages? Or, what unique qualities stand out in your mind about your child during early childhood? What is interesting to you about your child now?
6. Tell me of your observations of your child's beginning learning efforts (i.e., sitting-up, walking, talking, playing, etc.). Or, tell me

about early milestones, like sitting-up, walking, talking. Were any of these delayed?

7. All children have potential. Did you feel that _____ had some particular talent or "gift" early on? If so, what was it? What did your child do to make you think that he/she had this potential? Were there specific things you did as a parent to strengthen this talent?

8. What do you think your child might be when s/he grows up? Does your child know you think s/he will do this one day? Do you and your child talk about this talent?

9. Are there circumstances at home we should know about in school that may interfere with your child's learning at school? Please try to be as specific as possible in your response to this question.

Teachable Moments

10. Have you done anything around the house that your child saw or participated in that may have helped him/her learn something when s/he was younger? What was that "something"?

11. What are some of the ways that your child may have learned simply by watching you do something?

Homelife

12. How do you discipline your child? Does it work? Do you have certain "buzz words" that you use to get your child's attention? Have you shared these ideas with your child's teacher?

13. Tell me about your relationship with your child.

14. Are there any problems at home that might affect your child's interest in learning? Please be specific in your response to this question.

Educational Experiences

15. Does your child visit the public library? How often? Does he/she have a library card?

16. What type of summer activities does your child participate in?

17. Does your child participate in activities outside of school on a weekly or monthly basis? If so, what?

Parent's Beliefs about Their Child

18. What does your child want to be when he/she grow up? Do you believe he/she will reach that goal? What might prevent him/her from reaching their goal?

19. How does your child feel about school?
20. Is there something about your child that might not be obvious to the teacher, but might positively or negatively affect his/her performance in school if the teacher knew? If so, what would that something be?

Child's Time with Others

21. Who are the significant people in your child's life?
22. How much time would you say your child spends with other children? With other adults? How is this time usually spent?
23. Within the past week or two, what are some specific interactions that your child has had with you, his/her siblings, or adults that stick out in your mind? In the years past, what are some specific interactions that stick out in your mind?

Parent/Child/Sibling Relationship

24. What do you like about being a parent?
25. How do you view your role this year as a preschool, kindergarten, first, second, third-grade parent, etc.?
26. What would you like to have happen for your child in school this year?
27. What kinds of things do you do to help your child to be successful in school?
28. Do you and your family make things together at home? What kinds of projects have you done? What was this experience like?
29. Are both you and your spouse involved in your child's school learning? If so, how?

Parents' Hobbies, Activities, and Interests in Books

30. What activities/hobbies do you participate in as an individual? With your spouse or friends? As a family?
31. What kinds of books/magazines do you read? Did you read much when you were growing up? What kinds of books/magazines did you read as a child when you were growing up?

Parent/Teacher Relationship

32. What do you think your child's teacher could do to help you with your child's learning experiences at home?
33. Do you feel you can communicate your concerns about your child's learning with his/her teacher? How often do you and your child's teacher communicate with each other?

34. What methods of communication work best for you? In what ways do you usually communicate?
35. How could parent/teacher communication be improved?
36. What are some of the ways that you are involved in your child's school-learning experience?
37. In research articles that I've read, many researchers have found that children who have parents involved in school do better in school. What are your ideas on this research finding? What are your ideas about how parents and teachers could work together for the benefit of children and your child in particular?
38. If you could describe your child's teacher to another parent, how would you describe him/her?
39. If you could say something at the beginning of the year to a teacher that would communicate to him/her your wishes, desires, concerns, and fears for your child, what could you say to the teacher that would be very representative of _____?

Parent's School History—Ideas about School

40. If you could let your child's teacher know one thing that one of your own teachers did that strongly influenced you negatively or positively what would it be?
41. What do you remember about your own efforts to read and write? Was it difficult for you to learn to read? How did you learn to read?
42. Did your teacher(s) include or ask for your opinions and/or suggestions in designing what they taught? If so, provide some examples. If not, discuss why your teacher(s) chose not to include your opinions and/or suggestions.
43. Did you enjoy school? If not, when did you begin to dislike school? Can you remember what caused you to feel this way?
44. Can you describe your favorite teacher? What did you like most about him/her?
45. Can you describe your least favorite teacher? What did you dislike about him/her?
46. Can you describe your elementary, middle, or high school principal?
47. Can you describe the contact you've had with your elementary, middle, or high school principal?
48. Everybody has hopes and dreams when they are young children. As a child, what did you want to be when you grew up? Did that change over the years? Have you realized your childhood goals for your future?

49. Can you describe "something" about your home learning environment that you feel might be different from the learning environment of the school?

50. Can you describe "something" about your home learning environment that you would like the school to build upon because you feel that this "something" would enhance your child's learning potential at school?

WHAT TO DO WITH
WHAT YOU'VE COLLECTED

We hope that the questions on our questionnaire have given you some insight into the families and children you are working with this school year. In the next chapter we walk through the process of extrapolating salient information from conversations based on parent interviews. Further, we provide ideas that you can use to guide further conversations with parents and to develop instructional plans for students.

REFERENCES

Leichter, H. J. 1984. "Families as Environments for Literacy." In *Awakening to Literacy,* ed. H. Goelman, A. Oberg, and F. Smith, 38–50. Exeter, NH: Heinemann.

McGilp, J., and M. Michael. 1994. *The Home-School Connection: Guidelines for Working with Parents.* Portsmouth, NH: Heinemann.

Pearson, P. D. 1996. "Reclaiming the Center." In *The First R: Every Child's Right to Read,* ed. M. F. Graves, P. Van Den Brock, and B. M. Taylor, 259–274. New York: Teachers College Press.

4

Making Sense of Parent Stories

Yuou've collected one or more parent stories—now what do you do with all the information you've gathered? In this chapter we'll show you some ways to analyze and utilize the conversations that you've had with parents—step by step. Interspersed with our ideas are two parent story narratives that we collected through our conversational interviews with parents. Each story contains elements, which make it unique, but also demonstrate some of the commonalties that are found when parents talk about their home lives with their children. As you read each parent story narrative, imagine that the parent is sitting in front of you, telling you about their child and their family. What are your reactions? What are your initial ideas about how this information can be used to help each parent's child? Does what each parent says resonate with what you know about some of the parents you come into contact with?

You'll be on the path toward adding parent stories to the other tools that you use as a professional through using our ideas to read and respond to the parent story narratives in this chapter. By explaining not only what steps we suggest you go through to make sense of your parent stories, but also why we suggest these steps, we hope to provide you with the latitude to adapt and modify our ideas for your own use.

THE FIRST LANDMARK: WRITING YOURSELF A MEMO

By thinking about parent stories in specific ways, you will provide yourself with a "path" to follow that will guide you toward establishing a better understanding of the students and families with whom you work. We think of this path as having three important "landmarks." You've reached the first landmark when you write yourself a memo.

All of us are familiar with different kinds of memos—some are given to us by our principals or by the various committees that we might be a part of through our jobs. Other memos are written by us, to our families or ourselves. We use them to help remember things like picking up groceries or making phone calls. In other words, we use them to remind ourselves of the things we need to do or think about.

After you've had a conversation with a parent based on the information we gave you in the last chapter, we suggest that you write a memo to yourself about the conversation. This kind of memo is more detailed than the average grocery list, but its purpose is the same—to help you remember and think about the important aspects of the parent stories you collect through conversations with parents. In the following, we've provided you with an opportunity to practice writing a memo to yourself by using one of the parent stories that we've collected. First, read through the parent story. Then, write a practice memo and memos of your own using some of the questions we've written down.

As You Read: Some Notes

This parent story was collected through gaining answers to the questions asked in the last chapter. We've transformed the parents' answers into a running dialogue so that it reads the way it might have sounded. As you read, feel free to make notations in the margins, and underline important ideas and things that trouble you or that you have questions about.

PARENT STORY: ANGELA AND TIMOTHY SHEFFLAND

My name is Angela Sheffland. This is my son Timothy. He's the oldest, he's eight—no, seven, I'm sorry, seven (laughs).

I was a slow learner in school. I had to have special help when I was in school because I was behind on my reading, my writing, math, all that. My mom just said that I was the "slow one" pretty much. Cause I was slow at learning everything (laughs). I was tested, just like I've had Timothy Jay tested, and their dad, when he was growing up, he was slow. He needed the special help, too. Timothy is not slow; he just needs a little extra help. Uhm, I think it's more . . . when I was in school I had the special help from kindergarten all the way up; I had to go in for speech, I had to have the extra help with math to help me get going in math, all the way up to my senior year I had to have the extra help. I always thought it was because I was slow and I was behind everybody else. Other than that, I don't know the reason (laughs).

I do home interiors at night. I'm home in the daytime, but then two hours, anywhere between two to three hours a night, I'm not in the home. Usually seven to nine. So, I'm not there. They go to bed like an hour after I leave, at eight o'clock. So what they do, they do with their dad at that time. Timothy comes home at four. Uhm, we spend time about an hour after he comes home and then about two hours before they go to bed. On the weekends, he's with his brother and sister all day long. Once in a while he'll be with cousins, or other little friends, depending on the day and the time.

His grandparents, his aunts, one of his soon-to-be uncles next year, all of us keep kind of in the goal of learning his words and "keep on studying" and all that. He's trying to read. He's learning how to read. He's in the process of that. One day, he caught us all off guard and read a whole page all by his self. We really encourage that; we think that is one of the greatest things! I normally keep little storybooks around, and I always encourage him to pick them up. He made up his first story, "The Three Little Pigs and the Big Bad Wolf." He made his first story with that one so I kind of keep him encouraged on that because I always keep their storybooks out so that they can get to them if they want to read or look at the pictures. One day, he just sat down and made his own little story to it. I thought it was cute (laughs).

He was a very quiet baby. Never, I mean you never heard a cry out of him, nothing. He was a very quiet child. I don't know about now. I think he's sort of like, changed (laughs).

There was a lot of things he did when he was little that I remember—it's really sad when you can't remember one (laughs). Oh, he was one, and he was at that stage of biting. He would sneak up to you and bite you on the back of the leg, and catch you off guard. He was good at that. That was (laughs) one I always remember, about the biting. He learned how . . . when we was two, he started talking. He said, "stop it!" and "leave me alone." I think it's when he was biting everybody, we told him, "stop it, you don't do that!" He just more or less got "leave me alone" on his own, or heard it from someplace. But I think he's doing good (laughs).

We took him to a carnival when he was one and a half. I can't remember which one it was. I think it was Fourth of July, and then when he was six, we took him to the one when we lived up north (Northern Michigan). They had fun, him and his brother.

When his brother was three and one-half or four, he was in kindergarten. He had to repeat kindergarten again. But he would sit down, help his brother count, do colors, all that. He was doing really good. I think he might be a teacher, but it could change. I mean, one day he told me, "I'd like to be a teacher someday," and I was like "cool!" (Angela turns to Timothy and asks him a question) What would you like to be? What was it that you told Daddy you wanted to be? I can't remember. (Timothy answers "a policeman.") A policeman? You want to be a policeman?

I think that their dad gets them into Sega and stuff like that. It's funny because sometimes he can get his dad out of tight spots when it comes to Sega games. They play one game and he just, he goes "no, dad, go this way," and it gets him out of the cavern or wherever else.

He watches his dad more than he does me. What are some of things you learn from daddy? Playing Sega? (Laughs). I clean up after them in the living room area, but they have to clean up after themselves in keeping their room cleaned, but there's some days when they flat out refuse and won't do it, so there's days when I feel that I'm more or less falling behind by not getting them up there.

We was getting ready to move, and we was going through and packing up the house. They jumped in and helped us pack up everything in their room. I asked them to pack up their stuff in their room and they did a really good job of it. They . . . he listened. He helped his brother out and got it all packed up so we could move their room over to the new house. So, they really helped us out there. All I really had to do was show him once. I had to show his brother twice, but I only had to show him once and he caught on and helped me out on showing his brother how to pack up their toys and clothes and all that.

When I was helping his brother . . . I was helping him with his alphabets, it was his second year in kindergarten; I was helping him with his alphabets, and like normal kids, they just throw up their hands like "I don't want to do it anymore, forget it." And I told him he could go off and play with his brother. Timothy sat his brother down on the floor in the bedroom and was showing him how to write his alphabets. It was so cute. We caught him off guard (and he said) "Oh, I didn't do that Mom. You didn't see that." It was so cute.

We just went and seen Toy Story. We read stories or goof around, whichever comes first. We're always trying to find something to do for the weekend. It's trying to figure out something you can do with the kids, to keep them enthused, but also to get them to learn how to count and keep them counting and keep them up with schoolwork, too. I'm mainly trying to get him to learn everything that he can learn, keep his education first. Get it up there where he can reach his highest goal.

We make sure he does his homework every night if he has homework. If he don't have homework, he sits down and at least practices something that has to do with school, but other than that, as far as I know, there's nothing around the house that will make him not want to learn or anything.

He has the willpower to learn. He's trying, and that's one thing. We argue over homework. He just got his report card and he's doing better than what we expected he was doing. He's still behind a little bit, but like they said, he's trying his hardest and that is all we tell him to do is keep trying. The harder you try, the farther you'll go. We more or less have him sit down and we have him practice his spelling. He spells the words to us, he points them out to us and we just keep on top of his spelling so that he gets it all changed one way or another. His teachers have taught him to finger count, which is really good because he'll sit down and he'll count with his fingers. The first time he did that, I was like, "what are you doing?" I've never seen that before. And he goes, "I'm finger counting, Mom." He counted it out on his fingers and I was like, "cool! That's a new one!"

He learns best when it's kind of one-on-one. If there's a lot to be taught or if there's a lot of people or children in a room to be taught something, it's like he can't comprehend as easy as it is one-on-one. I've pretty much told his teachers because the one-on-one contact helped me a lot in school, and it's working out great for him. His teachers are really proud that he's catching on as fast as he is—as long as it's one-on-one he catches on and he knows what's going on that way, but if he has a whole group of kids in the room with him, he just will not learn.

We do plastic canvas, we paste and glue and work with beads and all that. He likes it, but then after a while, he sort of like gets bored with it. He'll do the arts and crafts fifteen to twenty minutes, but then after that, forget it. He's tired of it, he's all done; he's ready to go. His one teacher, not Mrs. Freedman, but the other one, Mrs. Lareau, right? She just tells me to sit down and go one-on-one with him, that way he learns everything that he should be learning and it's easier for him if I just sit across from him and just have the paper sitting in front of us and let him go that way. It's easier, and he gets a lot more down on paper than when it's a group situation. To me, I think he's just having trouble comprehending some of the work that he has to do. Because he can come home right now with a word and he knows it just like that, and it's weird because he goes through the stages, I mean phases, to where one minute he knows what he's doing and the next minute, it's like "I don't know," and you're like "you do know, because you just got through doing it for us." And it's, I tell him "don't be doing that. Because if you're doing this at home, I know you're doing this at school." It's . . . he knows what he's doing but he likes to play that he doesn't. And we know that he knows what he's doing (laughs).

We've been trying to figure out something for I don't know how long to keep him from going into "lala land," because he does it early in the morning, and he does it after lunch. And Mrs. Freedman is constantly saying "Timothy, do you remember what you're supposed to do when you first come in here in the mornings?" Cause he's supposed to, uhm, check in—they've got clothespins up at the front of the room with their names on them—they keep them on track of what they're supposed to do in the morning. They're supposed to get their drinks in the morning, go to the bathroom, and then sit down and take out their journal and write in it for the day. And he just don't do that. He just goes and sits down and says, "what am I supposed to do today?" If we could just get him to remember what he's supposed to do.

I try to get him to write his name, like Mrs. Freedman does. Uhm, and get him to check in and stuff like that. Take care of his coat. It's like it's in one ear and out the other one. We're trying to figure out something, but it's difficult because he just doesn't want to. When he has to go to bed at night for school in the morning, he throws a fit and he starts stomping his feet. He does it once in a while when he's having a bad day. I just reverse whatever he wants (laughs). It seems to work now. I just more or less say, "well, you know if you don't go to bed, you're not going to be refreshed so you can learn something new in school. And he looks at me like "Well, I'm going to bed, then." And I'm just like "okay, good night." And it will get him to go to bed for me.

I know that I should be coming in and spending time with his class to figure out more of what he's learning. Because he gets spelling words home and he brings home every Friday a storybook to read. I think I should come in and sit down a couple of times and watch and see what else he learns in school so I can go home and help him out at home with that instead of just leaving it up to the teacher to do. So . . . I've just about told his teacher everything (laughs). When he gets antsy, he gets antsy. It's like his attention span is real short, and he gets antsy, so he'll get up and disturb the other children in doing so. So I tell her to tell him that it's time for a time out. Have him sit down and read something for a few minutes or I tell her to just make him have a time out, because otherwise he'll just disrupt the whole class. Because he does it at home and we have to make him have a time-out period. "Sit down and take a chill" (laughs). That was her main concern was the antsy-ness like that because he's always up and around and into everything. We've more or less told him that his education is more important than anything else other than growing up, being a child. But always remember that his education should come first. Always learn as much as he can.

WORKSHEET ONE: WRITING YOURSELF A PRACTICE MEMO

Now that you've read through Angela's story and made some notes about it, we're going to walk you through a set of questions designed to help you think about and analyze what Angela has said.

1. Go back to the notes that you made about Angela's story. Which aspects of what she had to say were positive? Which were negative? Many times, it's easiest for us to identify the negative parts of what parents tell us. However, if we are to begin identifying and utilizing the strengths of parents and families, we have to work just as hard at finding the positive, no matter how hard it might be. Think about both the positive and negative things that you made note of in Angela's story and record them on a chart similar to Figure 4.1.

2. The second step in writing yourself a memo is to record the facts of the conversation—What happened at the beginning, middle, and end? By segmenting the conversation into these three parts and writing down your thoughts about these segments, you can begin to construct a picture of some of the more important ideas that the parent conveyed. Don't worry about being extremely specific—the point is to record the gist of the conversation. You may want to make notes on a chart like that in Figure 4.2 and refer back to Angela's story for confirmation of your notes.

Positive	Negative

Figure 4.1

Figure 4.2

3. Which of Angela's comments "stick out" in your mind? By this time, you'll have identified several ideas or themes, which seem to characterize her knowledge about her son. These are the kinds of ideas that will later help you to think about how you can organize activities for students that will help them socially and/or academically, while involving their parents. List the comments Angela made that "stick out".

4. After listening to Angela, what further questions do you have? One important aspect of parent stories is that they are simply a beginning point for organizing your conversations with parents. After initially talking with a parent, this conversation will likely raise other questions for you, which you might think about pursuing in subsequent conversations. So, list the questions that came to mind during and after you read Angela's story. Don't be politically correct! The objective is not only to figure out what questions you might ask if you were having a second conversation with Angela, but to figure out what kinds of information you think would be helpful in planning instruction involving Angela's son. By brainstorming a list of questions, you will be able to identify the kinds of information you feel are most important to obtain from individual parents. Use a heading such as:

Some Further Questions I Have Are:

WORKSHEET TWO: WRITING
YOUR OWN MEMO

Now that you've constructed a memo regarding Angela and Timothy, think about the parent(s) with whom you decided to talk. As soon as possible, write down your thoughts (or record them on an audiotape) about your conversation with each parent with whom you talked. Then:

1. Write down both the positive and the negative things that you heard during the conversation on a chart like the one shown in Figure 4.3.

2. Record the facts of the conversation—What happened at the beginning, middle, and end? Use a chart similar to Figure 4.4. You will want to review your audiotape or the notes that you made directly prior to the interview in order to complete the following sections.

3. What comments of the parent "stick out" in your mind? Record them briefly.

Positive	Negative

Figure 4.3

Beginning	
Middle	
End	

Figure 4.4

4. After listening to the parent, what further questions do you have? For example, were there things that puzzled you—information that you felt the parent was holding back or "editing"? Were there phrases that the parent used that you felt you needed further clarification on? Did you gain enough information about some of the experiences or activities that happen in the student's home? If not, what other questions might you ask?

Some Further Questions I Have Are:

There you have it—these notes that you've just made compose a "memo" to yourself about your conversation with the parent. Now that you have these notes, we hope that you can begin to see how they are an important step in understanding how you can "bridge the gap" between what goes on in your classroom and what happens when your students go home.

THE SECOND LANDMARK: BRAINSTORMING INSTRUCTIONAL IDEAS

So—you've talked with one or more parents, and you've also had an opportunity to construct a memo based on your conversations and your initial impressions. However, instead of feeling like a path is being cleared to understanding students and their families, you might feel as if you're cutting your way through a jungle of jumbled information. It's time for another landmark. What we'd like to do next is help you to look at the information you've gained in order to develop some instructional ideas that can help your student and involve their parent(s). We define instructional ideas as the general ways you can make sense of the information you've gained from parents in order to help your students in the classroom and support their learning at home. An instructional idea can be

- a short summarized version of something that a parent said about their child which seems like something you could use to help the child in the classroom
- one of the positive things a parent mentioned that you feel you could develop or work on
- one of the negative things a parent mentioned that you feel you might be able to alleviate or help the parent to deal with
- a brief idea about an activity or project that the parent or student could work on together
- ideas about how well the parent understands what's going on at school and notations on whether the parent needs to know more

These are just a few examples of what instructional ideas can be—feel free to use these examples to guide your own list of instructional ideas, but please also feel free to develop instructional ideas that go beyond what we've mentioned here.

To further help you understand both what instructional ideas look like and how to develop them, we've included a second parent story for you to read and respond to, and we've included some instructional ideas that we and other teachers came up with after reading the same parent story. After reading this second parent story and the accompanying instructional ideas, we would like you to brainstorm a list of instructional ideas that might be helpful to the students and parents that you've been working with.

PARENT STORY: HELEN AND JASON HARRISON

I'm Helen Harrison, and my son's name is Jason. I don't have too many hobbies outside home—I like to do flower arranging and crafts. As a family, we're basically homebodies really. We go to an occasional football game and basically stay around the home. Jason and I do basic, everyday, day-to-day things, and I play with him. We don't have a whole lot of excitement.

Jason doesn't—he's kind of afraid to do things. He likes to do things, and he's really good at things, but he's afraid to do them. He doesn't— he's afraid to do things. I think he'd be very good at playing hockey, but he's just afraid to go and try the challenge. He knows he's good, but he doesn't want to lose, I think. I think that's part of his "pull back." He just, you know, doesn't want to have anybody better than him. He likes to draw and he's pretty good at it. He's getting to be real good. He's looking at books now and copying what's in them, and during some—you know, just he's very inquisitive. He wants to know about everything, so . . . Like if something came up, uhm, oh, like last year there was an incident—it was lightning out, and he wanted to know where lightning came from and how it was and if it would hurt, and why it would hurt, and where you could be if it didn't hurt, and so most of my time is spent explaining things to him that he really needs to know in detail. You know, he doesn't stop at a quick answer.

When both my kids were young, they were very sick. I don't—they had a lot of ear infections; they both had pneumonia several times before they were like three. And so I can't say that we did a lot of things that were out-going that I remember. Nothing really stands out to me. There were every-day safety-type things, learning like that. Once him and his sister decided that it would be cool to, ah, light this piece of fuzz in the candleholder to see if it would burn. Well, it burned a lot better than they thought it was going to and they ran out and got me, "Mom, mom, the bathroom's got a fire in it," you know. They learned real fast that day that they don't light anything —even though I told them that, they don't light it. And Jason, to this day, does not like matches or anything lying around. So, you know just basically "live and learn" things like that.

One thing Jason did was when he was two, we lived in a townhouse at the time, and he was calling my name, and I walked to the front door, and he said "I'm stuck," and I said, "what are you stuck in?" And I looked at him and he was in the window well of a, you know, basement window. And I said, "Oh, Jason, get out of there," you know, "I don't have time to fart around and take you out." And he said, "No, but I'm stuck." And come to find out, he had stuck his foot down the drain tile. and he had rubber tennis shoes on, and when he went down into it, the shoe was kind of curved up like that, so he couldn't pull it out. And he was stuck there for almost two hours. I had to call 911, and then my dad come over and dug all this gravel out of this window well, and we got him jerked out of it, but you know, I was scared half to death, but I just remember him sitting there with the funniest look on his face and saying "No, I am; I'm stuck." I thought he was just playing because he always did that. I thought he was just sitting on his knee and come to find out he really was stuck!

What I think is interesting about Jason is that, like I said, you can't just answer him with a quick answer, because he wants to know how it works and why it works and what makes it run like that, so I think that's kind of interesting.

Our weekly routine is uhm, normal. I usually get him up at—I work full-time outside the home—I usually get him up at about twenty after six, give him breakfast, help him change his clothes, make his bed, get his stuff together for school for the next day if we haven't already done it. I have about fifteen minutes after all that to spend with him, and we usually talk about what he's going to do today, or he shown me what he's going to take to school. And then I drop him off at the sitter's, which is right down the street. And then he starts his day and I start mine. I like to get him to bed around nine o'clock. On a normal weekend Jason always wants to stay up late, and at this time of year he likes to watch every hockey game that comes on TV.

Like I said, he's not real outgoing. He doesn't want to join in a lot of activity things, so . . . he loves to play street hockey in our driveway, and he'll play for hours. But, I cannot get him to want to play on a team. But he loves to have neighbors come down and just play a little bit with him, and I don't know if it's the team, you know, if he's afraid of that, like I said, the challenge there will be too high for him, or what, but nope, he won't join.

I don't know if it's known, but Jason is—I'm divorced and remarried, uhm, my husband right now, we'd just like to see him gain better reading skills and he's very good at math, I think, but his reading skills are very poor, and so are my daughter's. So, you know, out of everything, I want to encourage him more to read. Because I think being the typical boy, he doesn't have time to read where my daughter had time to read—she just was unable. Jason really likes to read, but he really doesn't make the time. So, I think he's got to get a little bit older, plus I think it's kind of hard for him right now, so he'd rather just lay it aside, rather than to tackle it. But, uhm, his father, his real father, on the other hand, agrees that, well, he had a hard time in school, so that's the way it's going to be. So he's justifying why he's having a hard time. And basically, he doesn't have much to do with his schooling, and he's kind of supportive when Jason's around, like "you need to study, you need to do that"—but in real life, he, you know, when it comes to the conference, he says things like "Well, I had that problem, and he'll grow out of it."

I think the first few years for both my kids in the school they were going to, it was more social. There was more social problems there, and I don't think they got the help that they needed. Because they weren't "A" students or the teacher's pet or what have you. Uhm, I think they let them fall far behind. I really had to get them on my daughter; I basically had to tell them,

"Look, I don't agree with this report card. I don't agree with what you're telling me. I don't agree with any of it, because I don't see this happening." And the same way with Jason. Last year I had to just finally say, "Look, I want him tested for a disability, because I don't agree with this." When my daughter came home, or when I had went to her conference, they said "Oh, she's doing very well." They said, "You know, she's a little behind in that, but she's doing very well in school" and I looked at them and I said "She cannot even read a first-grade book, a sentence on the back of a cereal box, and she is in the third grade. I do not think she's doing that well." And I said I wanted her tested, even though everyone was saying "She loves to read, she loves to read." Well, what they finally found out was that she was somewhat dyslexic plus she didn't understand the way they were teaching it. The phonics just blew her away, and I think that's part of Jason's problem. They weren't getting it the way it was taught to them.

He's always—Jason's always known as—he's kind of on the hyper side, you know. He's not one to sit down for very long. So he runs around our basement and plays games while we all watch TV and stuff, and I guess the most comical thing—Jason really likes—and you never think he's paying attention to something, but he loves commercials. So, every time he's playing hockey around the basement or something, he'll stop, and he'll do a commercial. You know, he'll stop and spiel off some sort of commercial and it's kind of funny. And we all have to laugh at him, and then he goes back to playing like nothing was going on, but you know, he basically is pretty quiet other than that. I don't know what it is, but if a commercial catches his eye, he'll just keep doing it over and over, because he'll think it's funny. He memorizes commercials.

Jason is uhm, very easily influenced. He has some rowdy kids in his class, and he had come home and he told me that this teacher was going to call me. And I said "What for?" and he told me "Oh, because I tripped over a kid and he yelled that I hit him, and blah, blah, blah." I said "Okay, I'll just wait and see if the teacher calls me." Well, she called and left a message that simply said "Jason is picking on other kids, please talk to him." So I sat down and explained to him you know, that you have to be good in school, because if you don't be good in school, then you get sent to the principal's office, and then if you're really bad then you get sent home, and if you get sent home, then there's nobody there to teach you all of the reading and writing and the math, and all the stuff you want to learn. Plus there's no recess and there's no friends, and it really has a bad influence on you. And so I asked him after I got done with all that explaining if he understood what I had told him, and he said, "Well, I understood that I shouldn't be naughty in school." And I said okay. So the next day when he came home from school and he goes "Don't even ask me. Yes, I was good today." And I started laughing and I said, "Okay, I just wanted to know that." And he goes back and says, "Well, you don't have to ask me that every day, I told you I would be good." So I don't know, maybe I influenced him a little bit.

I don't know if Jason learns better in a group or more one-on-one right now. In certain things, he does really good in a group. Like he loves science and art as a group, because he can see what the other kids are doing or whatever. Reading—reading, I think he's a little shy, because he can't read as good as the other kids. He sat down and read me a few books last night that, you know, they were telling me that he's really kinda only reading a lower kindergarten/first-grade level, and he's in the second grade. But he read them real good for me. And I think he was so excited that he had read eight of them, and there are maybe ten pages in each. But he was so excited.

I don't have a whole lot of participation in the school, because I'm working all the time. I uhm, I sent a letter to them that if you need certain things cut out, or if you need items brought in, or if you need something from me, I'd be more than happy to come in, but, basically, you know, I can't get off my job and come in and help. Over the years, that's probably been the only thing that both of my kids have said "You never come in and help" because they have other mothers come in and help. Probably out of all the things that I can't do—you know, when they tell me that it's like "Well, gee you guys . . ."

Jason really needs to be—he can't be preoccupied with something, because if he's preoccupied over here, if some kid's making him laugh or something, he's just not going to stay in tune. And I think she's (the teacher) come to the same conclusions, because she's set him right up in front. To Jason, though, it wasn't that he got moved up front, it was that they'd turned their whole room into a letter "C" like his name. I said "Well, Jason, you know that she didn't really set you there because she wanted to create a letter of your name, she wanted you to sit right by her." I told him that and he goes "Yeah, well, I know that, but that's a "C." Plus a little girl that he likes was sitting right by him. And I started laughing and I'm like, well I hope it works for whatever she tried to do.

Jason's teacher didn't really ask me to share information about Jason at the beginning of the year. We came to the open house and stuff, and you know, it was so chaotic that they really didn't have much questioning. I felt kind of left out because she was all over the place and not really answering any questions . . . I just kind of wanted to know, you know, how he was doing at first, and what were the things that we're going to be doing. And it was more or less your typical open house. Uhm, this is where the kids stay, this is what they do . . . I'm not saying it was bad, I just think I would like to get it a little more structured where they'll say, maybe "This is our activities that we do through the day," and stuff like that. It was more or less "Hey mom, there's the computer I use," And "we do this sometimes," and then "Let's hurry up and go to my daughter's room." Which, when we got down there, it was the same thing. So I think it's part of your open house, trying to, you know, put a lot into it, and you don't have a lot of time. So I didn't really blame it on the teacher.

A lot of people used to think that if you, you know, got divorced that it would hurt the child, but for my two, I don't think it fazed them one way or another, because I kept in very good contact with my first husband. Uhm, he was able to come over anytime, he, uhm, he became very ill while we were separated—he got cancer. And I think that the fear of them seeing him go through all the cancer stuff was worse than our divorce ever was.

So, you know, I tried to work with them and let them know that it was going to be okay, but I think that for a while they were really unsure if their dad was going to be around, so I think they were preoccupied with that for about a year.

GETTING READY TO BRAINSTORM INSTRUCTIONAL IDEAS

What did you think about what Helen had to say? As we said previously, we shared Helen's parent story narrative with several other teachers and together we brainstormed a list of general "instructional ideas"—we've included some of these ideas below.

Instructional Ideas

- find out why he doesn't want to play hockey but enjoys it so much-Where is his fear of failure coming from?
- explore possibility of diet making him "hyper"
- connect learning with fire safety—Jason will probably feel able to contribute to class's understanding because of his experience when he was younger
- combine reading and writing with science (an area of interest for Jason)
- Mom needs to know that Jason does have time to read
- talk to her and Dad about self-fulfilling prophecies
- work from Mom's sense of organization in order to plan things for Jason to do at home

- make sure Jason is reading materials that aren't too hard. Needs to experience success
- Mom needs a better understanding of what teachers are doing and why—help her follow-up on what's happening in school
- make sure that any suggestions involve both Helen and her ex-husband (if at all possible)
- Jason likes details, and finding out the details about things—develop some ideas for projects that Helen can do with him at home and then share at school (make sure these projects involve some reading and writing). Maybe the teacher can involve Jason's interest in hockey, or TV commercials?
- get on a schedule in which Mom calls every so many weeks or receives a progress report so that she knows how Jason is doing and what she can do to help.
- Ask Mom if she can limit Jason's TV watching, especially if this is taking the place of possible reading he has to do for school.

Now, look back at the memo that you've made about your conversation with a parent. You've written down the positive and negative things mentioned in the conversation. You've also written down an account of what happened at the beginning, middle, and end. Finally, you've noted things that "stuck out" to you, and aspects of what the parent said that have led to further questions in your mind. Using all of these sources of information that you've created, you can brainstorm about your own instructional ideas in a notebook or a chart like that shown in Figure 4.5.

BRINGING IT ALL TOGETHER: CONSTRUCTING PLANS AND ACTIVITIES

The last landmark on your way to making sense of the parent stories that you collect involves taking the instructional ideas that you brainstorm and developing these into plans and activities that you can implement with the student (and parent). Once you've developed these ideas, you may find that you'll want to use them with more than just one or two students.

In the following we've taken two of the instructional ideas from the previous list and have added some detail to them so that you can see how they might be developed into more detailed plans and activities to use with Jason.

- Instructional Idea #1: Find out why he doesn't want to play hockey but enjoys it so much—fear of failure?

List Your Instructional Ideas in the Spaces Below	List the Sources of Your Instructional Ideas Below (This will help you keep track of where your instructional idea originated)

Figure 4.5 Brainstorming Instructional Ideas

Plans and Activities:

Perhaps it might be possible to have one of the hockey players from a local high school come in and talk to the class—either as part of a unit on different kinds of sports, or specifically to talk with Jason about his interest in hockey. The teacher could subtly provide an opportunity for Jason to talk about his love of hockey, and why he is reluctant to join an organized team, or the teacher could tell Jason about the visit beforehand and ask him if he would like to talk about his own participation in the sport of hockey.

Another related idea would be to have the students in the classroom do group projects about different kinds of sports (and assign Jason to the "hockey group"). Each group could do some artwork and reading/writing related to the sport and present it to the rest of the class. Perhaps each group could even demonstrate some of the aspects of the sport they are to discuss. This would give Jason an opportunity to do reading and writing related to hockey and he could possibly demonstrate (in his own words) some of the "fundamentals" of hockey to his classmates.

- Instructional Idea #2: Make sure Jason is reading materials that aren't too hard; he needs to experience success. Also, Mom needs a better understanding of what teachers are doing and why—help her follow-up on what's happening in school

Plans and Activities

In regard to Jason's reading and writing, the first step is to find out what reading materials Helen thinks are appropriate for Jason—the teacher needs to ask her to bring in some of the specific books that Jason has read or has tried to read lately. Once this information is known, the teacher can suggest other books that might be more appropriate. This conversation can help to make Helen more involved with what's going on with Jason at school, particularly if the books that the teacher suggests are ones that may be used in future lessons.

Additionally, the teacher can begin corresponding with Helen regularly —perhaps every two or three weeks. In this correspondence, the teacher can give Helen ideas about what Jason has been doing, as well as what he will be doing in the coming weeks. At this time, the teacher can also give Helen suggestions on ways she can help Jason be more successful with the work he will be doing. One note—Helen might be apprehensive or defensive about talking with the teacher, since she had to have "extra help" in school . . . this might be a perfect situation for some role playing, in which the teacher who will be talking to Helen practices a conversation with another teacher.

Your Turn!

We hope that these examples of plans and activities have been helpful to you. Using two or three of the ideas from your brainstormed list of instructional ideas, we'd like you to develop some plans and activities of your own in the following space, or in your notebook. We know that it may seem difficult to come up with some of these on your own, but we also know that you are creative and innovative enough to do it. So go ahead—give it a try! If you find that you're having trouble, we suggest that you collaborate with a colleague whose ideas and judgments you trust. Once you've written some plans and activities down, you can share them with another teacher and see what they think.

CONCLUSION

We hope that the ideas and activities of this chapter have been helpful to you. As always, our ideas for how to use parent stories are just a beginning point. We know that you may adapt or revise some of the ideas that we've presented to you. In fact, we encourage you to use our book in this way. You know your students best—and you are the one who has collected parent stories from your students' parents. Therefore, you are the final authority in terms of how to use the information that you've collected.

In the course of collecting parent stories, it's possible that what some parents tell you will go beyond what you can do as a teacher, and it is up to you to determine when this occurs. If you are in doubt, we suggest that you talk with another teacher. If you come to the decision that what a parent has said is indeed beyond the scope of what you can do as a teacher, we present some ideas for you in the next chapter. In Chapter 5, we suggest some ways that you can construct a resource file composed of community services and agencies that you might share with parents.

5

Implications of Parent Stories

While there are many positive things that can happen through im-
proved communication, when you start to get to know your students'
families better, you may run into more than you bargained for. Illiter-
ate parents, drug abuse, physical and sexual abuse, psychological prob-
lems, physical needs not being met, neglectful parents, will probably
be more than you can handle as a teacher. Be prepared to make refer-
rals to agencies that are better equipped to deal with those problems.

—Claire Batt, *Montessori Teacher*

OPENING THE LINES
OF COMMUNICATION:
ADDRESSING CONCERNS

Claire's words allude to issues that cannot be handled by schools and teachers
alone, as well as summarize fears that many teachers may have about opening
conversations with the parents of the children they teach because of what they
may learn. Low maternal education attainment, drug abuse, and absent fathers are just a few of the struggles represented by the three families in this
book. These parent stories force our minds to envision other people's realities
that do not fit into our schema of "family," "child," "community," or "school."
Most of us have not personally experienced abuse, drug addiction, and home-
lessness nor do we spend our idle minutes imaging ourselves in such dreadful
scenarios. Likewise, the potential for proximity to these issues via the children
attending day care centers, preschools, elementary, middle, and high schools
arouses uncomfortable feelings to say the least. This discomfort, however,

should not become a vehicle for dismissal of the existence of incredible stress in the lives of the children who enter classrooms every day. Instead, teachers and schools must devise a system that will aid families in need while protecting themselves legally, financially, and emotionally. Parent stories provide an avenue for conversation between parents and schools. Parent stories also help us to design community resource packets tailored to each family's unique set of circumstances and needs.

HOW TEACHERS CAN SEEK HELP AND REFERRALS OUTSIDE THE SCHOOL BY CREATING A RESOURCE FILE

Angela Sheffland, Mattie Howard, and Helen Harrison's parent stories present a range of problems and struggles that clearly and directly affect the school/ educational success of the children. On the one hand, we cannot ignore the impact that these issues have on children. On the other hand, schools and teachers cannot shoulder direct and total responsibility for all of the ills exposed in this book and in classrooms around the country. Teachers can and should prepare themselves to delegate problems out of their expertise by creating a "Resource File." The file contains information on a variety of local, state, and national resources for parents and families. The Resource File is a self-generated computer and/or hard-copy binder of community resource agencies that teachers utilize to delegate responsibilities that fall outside of their own duties.

The organization and framework that follow illustrate how we completed our own resource file. This particular approach worked best for us, but in order for a Resource File to be useful to you or your school, the format must be personalized to meet your needs.

PHASE 1.   Gather information on children in your classroom and their parents.

- Step 1. Making observations, collecting informal data
- Step 2. Interviewing parents: obtaining their parent stories

PHASE 2.   Gather information on resources in the community, state, and nation.

- Step 1. Recording resources known to you and locating additional resources

PHASE 3.   Assemble and distribute the information.

- Step 1. Assembling the completed Resource File and making information available to parents

PHASE 1— GATHERING INFORMATION ON FAMILIES

The first step in creating a Resource File is gathering information about the families who would be served by your file. It is important to target effort and energy toward appropriate resources. In other words, do not waste time in Phase 2 collecting information on Jewish Community Centers if you teach in a predominantly Catholic school.

Materials

Some materials that might be helpful, but *not* absolutely necessary include:

- method to record and date observations (tape recorder, file folders, three-ring binder, self-adhesive notes, etc.)
- file for each student/family in which to gather information

PHASE 1, STEP 1— OBSERVATIONS

Most teachers learn about their students through observation, a careful system of watching the children interact with classmates, adults, and materials as well as through one-on-one conversations with the children themselves. These observations are critical to the assessment of the child's current achievements. Knowing each child's current level in all areas of development is pivotal to employing Vygotsky's theory on the "zone of proximal development." Teachers need to implement a similar strategy in piecing together parent stories.

Before scheduling parent story conferences with parents, gather data informally. For example: How does the parent interact with the child when they are together? How does the parent interact with other adults? How comfortable does the parent seem in the school environment? What emotions are felt in informal conversations with the parent—fear, anger, distrust happiness, satisfaction, helplessness, and despair? In the general community, is the parent part of the majority or minority population in terms of race, ethnicity, SES, educational attainment level? In the school community, is the parent part of the majority or minority community based on the preceding criteria?

Valuable information may be gained about the parent's communication style, concerns, or topics, which generate strong emotions through your observations. This information will help you to select interview questions from our list as well as create pertinent questions of your own. Consider parent stories as you would any other professional interview—do your homework ahead of time to maximize information gained during direct interaction.

In addition to watching families, teachers should also explore the community in which they teach, especially if they reside in a different community. Teachers need to acquire a sense of how a community is organized, what the values and prominent belief systems are, what people do in their leisure time, etc. It may be helpful to shop for groceries, dine in a "local" restaurant, attend local theater productions, and spend an evening at the county fair. Through this primary research collection, teachers can build a schema of their own through which their interactions and conversations with parents will gain greater meaning and relevance.

PHASE 1, STEP 2 — PARENT STORIES

Now that you have gathered your informal data and used it to select and create interview questions for the parent, you are ready for the parent stories. Consider the location of the interview. Perhaps a neutral, safe location such as a restaurant or coffeehouse would provide both you and the parent a comfortable setting. Schools and classrooms often bring out negative memories from the parent's own school experience which could inhibit their openness. Conversely, you may not want to step into a stranger's home, alone. Keep two objectives in mind when choosing a locale: Be sensitive to the parent's need for privacy and, above all, be safe.

PHASE 2 — GATHERING INFORMATION ON RESOURCES

The next step is to gather information on local, state, and national organizations that would benefit your families based on your observations and parent story interviews collected and organized in Phase 1. Phase 2 has one step: Recording resources known to you and finding and recording resources unknown to you.

Materials

Some materials that might be helpful, but *not* absolutely necessary include:

- community phone books
- pencil/paper
- telephone
- long distance access code, if calling from work

PHASE 2, STEP 1 — RECORDING RESOURCES KNOWN AND UNKNOWN TO YOU

Begin by checking the government and yellow pages in the phone book, childcare referral networks (a gold mine for community resource information; if your own or any community around you has one, call them first), the internet, the chamber of commerce, hospitals, museums, art councils, bureaus,

YMCA/YWCA programs, and local shelters and food banks for leads. Compile phone numbers and addresses for all organizations and add to your Resource File.

Many community organizations are a wealth of information about other community organizations that offer similar resources. Continue to add to the file and call resources until you believe that there are enough resources to form a complete, diverse Resource File. Collect pamphlets, fliers, brochures, etc. in one central bin to facilitate removal of duplicate copies of information.

PHASE 3 — ASSEMBLY AND DISTRIBUTION OF THE FILE

This is the final step in the development of the Resource File. There is one step to complete the process: Assembly and distribution of information collected.

Materials

Some materials that might be helpful, but *not* absolutely necessary include:

- computer with spreadsheet program and/or
- three-ring binder
- sheet protectors in which to store pamphlets
- tabbed dividers

PHASE 3, STEP 1 — ASSEMBLING THE RESOURCE FILE AND DISTRIBUTING THE INFORMATION

Assemble the information alphabetically by category. In the three-ring binder, create a Table of Contents with cross-references and use tab dividers between sections to make your Resource File easy to use. Use clear, sturdy sheet protectors to visibly store information received from agencies.

It is also important to realize that some families may not request information because of pride or fear. Periodically send home universal flyers, which provide an array of information on both enrichment and crisis services. Explore the possibility of posting the flyer in community locations, extending the usefulness of services beyond the direct school-family dyad. During open houses, daily pick-up, conferences, any time parents are near your door, post a photocopied packet of information with a sign that says "Please Take One." If the invitation is there to take the information without the stigma associated with some of the topics included in the packet, parents may be more likely to receive information. If your school is equipped with voice mailboxes that include outgoing messages on topics ranging from homework assignments to lunch menus, investigate using a mailbox for posting your resources. If your school has a web site, post information on community resources there as well. The idea is to help the parent, through providing information in non-confrontational ways, believe that he/she has thought of this idea on his/her own. Ownership of an idea ensures greater success in the completion of that idea.

A SAMPLE FROM OUR OWN PARENT STORIES: USING COMMUNITY RESOURCES TO PROVIDE INFORMATION ON SERVICES TO THE HOWARD FAMILY

The families presented in this book demonstrate a range of needs. From the parent interviews, one can construct a resource packet for each family. Since we do not have informal observations from the teachers of the children presented in this book (*Phase 1, Step 1*), we will need to rely solely on the parent stories to construct a list of valuable resources (*Phase 1, Step 2*). Let's use Mattie Howard's story of her son Damon to compile a list of community resources. From the transcript of the interview, we will begin by compiling a list of comments and possible resources (*Phase 2, Step 1*) that may be of interest to Mattie.

PARENT STORY: MATTIE AND DAMON HOWARD

I'm applying for a job to work with the kids in the lunchroom getting their lunches together and making sure they act right in the lunchroom. Then they have an after-school program from three thirty to seven p.m. and I'll just be there with the kids and they have to eat and you work with them and do different things with them, so I'm going to see if I can do that. But until then, I'm still going to be cleaning, you know, until I find out if I get the job. But if I don't, I still like being there because I'm there from eleven in the morning until two, and then I go back at five thirty in the evening and I'm there until eight thirty. I'm there with the students all day, and the teachers, and they're real nice, and it's like a family thing up there and I really like it.

I do a lot of bowling. I'm not that good, but I like it. And my sisters and my next door neighbor and I go out maybe two nights a week and play pool. I really don't have a lot of friends, my sisters are my friends and we just do everything together. We're really close to each other—not next door, but in the area, we're not far from each other at all. I have a twenty-one year old daughter and she participates with us a lot. At home right now it's just me and my son Damon. I have a twelve year old, but he stays with his father down south, and my twenty-one year old, she's on her own in her own place.

Damon loves Nintendo. We sit there and play that a lot. We also go to the putt putt course together, and we go out to eat a lot together. Basically around the house we do a lot of things together. He has a lot of different games and I'll play them with him. Then I work with him with his home-work and different words, because he's having problems with his reading. I've made flashcards and I try to play little games with him with the flash-cards. Damon gets upset when I'm trying to teach him a word and he doesn't know it. He really gets upset and it kind of makes me mad, because I know he can do it if he tries, so I try to like, maybe rap with him with the words or something like that to make it kind of fun for him to want to do it. It works a little bit, because at first I was just working with the flashcards and it wasn't working. Then Mrs. Carr told me "Well Mattie, try something a little fun with the words and maybe he'll show more interest in it." And now he's kind of showing a little bit more now.

I remember when Damon was about one years old, and I took him to his first carnival down at the riverfront—he enjoyed being on the rides. We did a lot when Damon was around three or four. Like I said, we didn't really do much other than go to different putt putt courses and we always did stuff like that because I like to play video games myself. They have this game called "Bart Simpson" and Damon likes that one. And they have this other one that's something like a slot machine, because I go to a nearby casino sometimes, I play that game quite a bit. I like that one. When we're at home now, because Damon is doing bad in school I do my normal thing of fixing something to eat, and we work on his spelling words. That what I'm on with him real bad. I think he has difficulties in spelling. The thing with Damon is that he really doesn't try. I could put a word in front of him like "the" and then ask "Damon, what is this word?" and he'll just look, he'll try to sound it out, but when he says it, it comes out to be something entirely different. It frustrates me because I don't want him to repeat the first grade again. I don't. And I know he can do it, because he was doing well before Christmas vacation, and when he came back from that, it seemed like he just forgot everything.

The most interesting thing about Damon is that he's really spoiled. Very. It's because I try to do everything for him, because I didn't spend enough time with my other two kids that I had like I'm spending with him now. I didn't spend as much time with my other children because I had my first child at a very young age, and she was left with my mother, and I was wild, you know, going on mean street. And then my son, I kept him maybe up to about four years old, then his dad moved away and he wanted him, so I let his dad take him, because again, I really wasn't ready for kids. I was much older when I got pregnant with Damon and I think my other kids noticed because I didn't give them that attention like I should have, and I'm not going to go that route again, so I just try to do everything I can for Damon. When I had my daughter I was fifteen, and when I had my first son, I was in my early twenties. And I was thirty-two when I had Damon, so it's a big difference.

My usual routine is to get up and get Damon ready for school. I go back home and I do a little house cleaning, and then I go to work at eleven. And then I'm home at two. I sit down for a little while, and then I have to be up at the school at three to pick Damon up. Then, like I said, I'll go home and fix him something to eat. Then I work with him on his schoolwork for a little while. Then I let him go to his room and play Nintendo. Then I might take a nap, and I'm ready to go back to work around five thirty. That's five days a week. On Saturdays Damon is on that Nintendo. I think that he's on that Nintendo too much, but he's on the Nintendo on weekends. Then we might go over to my sisters' and he plays, because my two sisters have sons and they're all around the same age. Damon's dad isn't involved in his life—he doesn't stay here in town. His father was into drugs so I got away from that. Since he was four, Damon has never seen his father—just once I took him to see him. His father wanted to keep him but I knew what kind of life he was living, so I let him visit while I was there, but other than that, Damon's never seen him. He doesn't talk about him or anything. I did have another male friend, but I think he was kind of jealous of me and Damon's relationship, because he would always ask me why I let Damon do certain things that he didn't think I should. Damon really didn't care too much for him, so he'll be going soon, because I already know who comes first.

I want Damon to make it all the way through school, because I didn't. Well, I did make it through the twelfth grade, but I didn't graduate. I want him to graduate. I want him to go to college. If he doesn't, I want him to at least find a good job, you know, and be set in his ways to be able to take care of himself if something ever happened to me. I want to make sure that he's going to be taken care of, that he'll be able to take care of himself. I want him to make it through school. I really do. I really do.

Damon has done some things that I worry about. I was getting him ready for school a couple of days ago, and he had this toy gun sitting on the dresser. And I saw him pick up the gun, and I said "You're not taking that to school. Put that back." And he said, "Okay, I'm not going to take it." The next day they called up to my job and talked to my sister, because she works up there, and said that Damon brought a toy gun to school. And when Mrs. Carr asked him was it his gun or another boy's, he lied and said it wasn't his gun. When the principal got him in her office, and asked him to tell her the truth, he started crying and said that it was his gun. And I was just kind of sick with that. I don't like him to lie. I don't like it at all. He does kind of lie a lot. I don't know why he does it, because like I said, I'd do anything for Damon. When I see the tears coming, I know that he lies. And he lies a lot. I don't know why he does it, I think it kind of comes from his dad's side. And then I think he does it because he can't really think he's scared I'm going to whip him, because that's what a lot of my family says my problem is. I don't whip him, because I don't really like hitting him. I might yell at him, or I'll take away something from him that he really likes, like his TV that's in his room.

Another time I had five dollars sitting on my jewelry box, and I went to get the five dollars, and it was gone. And he had this little power ranger wallet that I had bought him. And I asked him, "Damon, have you been in my room?" I said "You didn't see any money in my room?" And he said "No." I went in his room and looked through his drawers and found his wallet and my five-dollar bill was in there. I said "Damon, why do you lie?" and it's always "I don't know, I don't know."

Damon likes to help me clean. In the mornings he'll try to make up his own bed. It might not be right, but he does try, and he puts his stuff back in place. I guess he sees me do it a lot. He'll stack his shoes up right; he'll uhm, put all his toys and stuff back in place. He'll try to make up his bed. He'll hang his coats up on hangers and put them in the closet. He can put clothes in the washer, and he likes to put the soap inside the washer, and he'll help me fold. He just very much likes to always help me. Sometimes I take him to work with me, and he'll go around to all the classrooms and he'll get the trash from the trashcans and he'll dump them. I always tell him that if you see a bag that has something sticky inside it, don't just dump it and put it back, let me know so I can change the whole bag, and now he doesn't even let me know; he just changes the bag himself.

Right now he wants to be a power ranger, and I try to tell him that it's not real. That's another reason why I'm trying to stop him with the television so much, because he's into it a whole lot. If I had to hypothesize about what he might be, I would say, like a basketball player. In the summer when my brother comes over a lot and takes him to the park, he finds a good interest in that when my brother takes him.

I think Damon learns best when I'm constantly on him about something. He won't really learn by sitting there and watching it himself. Someone has to be there to kind of, you know, edge him on. Like for instance, his homework. When he comes home with his homework, I like to let him try to go by himself first. And when he's in his room trying to do it by himself, I could hear him in there talking to himself. You know, "I can't do this. I can't do this. I'm going to go out there and ask mom to do it." You see, he wants me to come out and just do it. But I told him that I can't do that, because if I do it, he would never learn how to do it. I don't know why he thinks he can't do it. I really don't know. I think it's that Nintendo, I really do. Now he can play that like I don't know what. He's really good at it. And I don't want to take it away from him completely because I know he really likes it.

I like shopping for him. You know, I like dressing him, because I like to keep him up real well. And you know, fixing his dinners and talking to him about different things like that, you know? I talk to him about what I want him to be when he grows up. I talk to him about one day I might not be here, and "What would you do if I'm not here? Would you go on with your life and try to be something?" He never tells me what he's going to do if something were to happen to me and I'm gone. All he says is "I don't want you to go and you're never going to go."

1) *Mattie says: "I'm applying for a job to work with kids in the lunchroom . . . but until then, I'm still going to be cleaning . . ."*

Analysis and Possible Resources

Is Mattie happy doing this kind of work? She seems to be articulate and to have a clearer sense of herself now that she is older. Is going back to school to get her GED then to community college or vocational school a possibility for her? Perhaps gather information on adult education classes, vocational education, and community college programs in your area.

2) *Mattie says: "I have a twelve year old . . . [who] stays with his father . . . and my twenty-one year old, she's on her own in her own place. . . . Damon is really spoiled . . . I try to do everything for him because I didn't spend enough time with my other two kids . . . I didn't spend as much time with my other children because I had my first child at a very young age . . . and I was wild . . . going on mean street . . . and then my son, I kept maybe up to about four years old, then his dad moved away and he wanted him, so I let his dad take him . . . I really wasn't ready for kids."*

Analysis and Possible Resources

Does Mattie feel guilty about her past decisions, would she benefit from counseling in order to move forward and make positive steps as a parent for Damon? Are there family service organizations in your community who offer group or individual counseling; private counselors who volunteer their expertise to low income individuals?

3) *Mattie says: "I do a lot of bowling. I'm not that good, but I like it . . . I really don't have a lot of friends, my sisters are my friends and we just do everything together."*

Analysis and Possible Resources

Mattie enjoys bowling; would she enjoy other sport-based outlets (softball, volleyball, tennis, etc.)? Does your community have a community center, YMCA, or YWCA where Mattie could pursue current and additional interests? Would Mattie like to broaden her emotional resources beyond her immediate family? Perhaps your school/school system or local community centers offer mixers or programs (hiking, bowling, cooking, etc.) that would offer opportunities to meet new people with common interests.

4) *Mattie says: "Damon loves Nintendo . . . On Saturdays Damon is on that Nintendo. I think he's on that Nintendo too much, but he's on the Nintendo on weekends . . . we also go to the putt putt club together [to play video games] . . . I like to play video games myself . . . he has a lot of different games and I'll play them with him . . . Then I work with him with his homework and different words, because he's having problems with his reading . . . I think he has difficulties in spelling . . . I've made flashcards and I try to play little games with him with the flashcards . . . I think Damon learns best when I'm constantly on him about something. He won't really learn by sitting there watching it himself."*

Analysis and Possible Resources

Does Damon need tutoring in some content areas to catch up? Does your school or community offer special education programs for which he qualifies? A peer tutoring (by older children) program? After school tutoring? Do his problems warrant a certified tutor? Do Damon and Mattie need ways to enjoy time together other than playing video games? Investigate parent/child programs sponsored by the public library, YMCA, YWCA, school, or community centers.

5) *Mattie says: "Damon gets upset when I'm trying to teach him a word and he doesn't know it. He really gets upset and it kind of makes me mad, because I know he can do it if he tries . . . The thing with Damon is that he really doesn't try . . . It frustrates me because I don't want him to repeat the first grade again . . . I know he can do it because he was doing well before Christmas vacation, and when he came back*

from that, it seems like he just forgot everything . . . [in addition]
Damon has done some things that I worry about . . . He does kind of
lie a lot . . . And I was just kind of sick with that."

Analysis and Possible Resources

Mattie believes that Damon's educational problems stem from a lack of effort, not a lack of intelligence or skill. Also, he has begun to exhibit behaviors (lying) that Mattie does not like and does not know how to address. Does your community offer parenting programs and groups where Mattie could hear concerns from other parents, many of whom will have similar worries? Revisit the special education or tutoring services that might be available. Could Mattie learn the techniques used in such programs to reinforce what and how Damon is learning in school at home?

6) *Mattie says: "Damon's dad isn't involved in his life—he doesn't stay*
   here in town. His father was into drugs so I got away from that. Since
   he was four, Damon has never seen his father."

Analysis and Possible Resources

Does Mattie believe that Damon needs a male role model? If so investigate the Big Brothers program in your area. Also, some community centers or YMCAs offer programs that would be run by adults from whom Damon could learn. Another worry is that Mattie has children by three different fathers one of whom has been involved in drug use. Are there free women's health and STD/AIDS testing and education clinics nearby?

7) *Mattie says: "Right now he wants to be a power ranger . . . that's an-*
   other reason why I'm trying to stop him with he television so much . . .
   if I had to hypothesize what he might be, I would say . . . a basketball
   player . . . he finds a good interest in that when my brother takes him."

Analysis and Possible Resources

Mattie and Damon are falling into a classic pattern of setting unrealistic lifetime goals. It is impossible for Damon to be a power ranger, and extremely unlikely that he will become a basketball player. Local recreation programs and the YMCA may offer opportunities to mingle with other youth and adults in a positive, safe environment. These experiences will help build self esteem and provide eye-opening "reality checks."

After analyzing and brainstorming possible resources, compile a list of resources (*Phase 3, Step 1*) on which you could gather information. For Mattie, the compiled list of resources would be:

- adult education/GED programs
- community colleges
- vocational education programs
- family services counseling
- general counseling or therapy groups
- public library
- community centers
- YMCA
- YWCA
- parent education classes, seminars, groups
- special education programs—school based
- tutoring programs: peer, after school, certified private tutor
- Big Brothers and Big Sisters
- women's health clinic
- STD/AIDS testing and education clinic

Once you have collected several information packets or fliers from local, state, or federal associations/groups design a method or methods of distribution (*Phase 3, Step 1*) which you think will be most effective and reach the largest number of families regardless of how many parent stories you decide to do. As previously mentioned, creating "send home" packets, posting information freely outside your classroom, on an outgoing voice mail message, or on your schools website are just a few ways to reach families in your classroom.

CONCLUDING COMMENTS: TRYING PARENT STORIES AND CREATING THE RESOURCE FILE ON YOUR OWN

For good reason, many of us are hesitant about approaching parents with suggestions of services outside the school that parents might want to utilize. We do not want to be perceived as meddling in affairs that are none of our business, or as being condescending or judgmental of parents. However, the fact remains that many families could benefit from services that different agencies and organizations can provide. In dealing with this dilemma, we must be creative. One idea that has promise is to use the resource file as a source for information that can be included in parent newsletters to highlight the services provided by different agencies and organizations. Each month, a different agency or organization could be highlighted in the newsletter, and questions could be included in the newsletter so that parents could begin to think about whether the agency or organization might be helpful to them. For example, a newsletter highlighting different sports-related organizations could include questions such as "Does your son/daughter seem to have lots of excess energy that you want to channel?" and "Would you like your son/daughter to have the opportunity to be in a learning environment, while at the same time developing physical skills?" The newsletter could then go on to describe the various organizations that are available in the community, along with sources of aid for families who might not be able to afford the fees attached to involving their children in sports. Once newsletters like this have been disseminated, teachers could simply include them in a packet of information to be given out during parent-teacher conferences.

Even after we have considered how to approach parents with community resources and we have devised ways to disseminate the information, completing the actual resource file can seem like a daunting task. Therefore, we advise that you leave yourself open to the possibility that you might create such a file gradually, over the course of a year or even two. Furthermore, we suggest that you might want to work with one or two other teachers in completing the file, so that you can collaborate with each other and modify it so that other teachers can find it useful.

Before beginning with a "real" family from your own classroom, you might want to try to glean some critical comments from either Angela or Helen's parent stories. Create your own analysis and brainstorm about the possible resources that Angela or Helen could access if they lived in *your* community. Compile a complete list. It is often surprising how many resources a single family could utilize!

After you feel relatively comfortable with the process, start small in your own classroom. Select two or three families to "test drive" the entire process of gathering pertinent parent stories and constructing valid, Resource Files for each. Each year, as you become more confident and refined in your collection and analysis skills, you will be able to add more families to your list. Ultimately it would be wonderful to have parent stories and Resource Files for every child in your class.

EPILOGUE—Joining Hands on the Path

We think that the metaphor of paths that are both beginning and ending aptly describes what we wanted to achieve in writing this book and what we wanted those concerned with education to be able to do with the book once it was written. In some ways, the process of putting this book together symbolizes the end of a path that began when the research project on parent stories was first conceptualized. In the process of completing the project, we (at all times) had our eyes on the ability of the project findings to have implications for those who have struggled to be able to value parents' knowledge and use that knowledge for constructive purposes. It was not always clear how the information we gained from parents would be applicable to the issues and problems that educators face. After all, the information that parents were telling us was clearly sensitive, and in many cases the information that they volunteered could have been used to substantiate the "inadequate" home environments in which many children live. Despite this fact, we continued to work on ways in which parents' information could be critically but *caringly* used to aid in the instruction and development of students in classrooms—and we enlisted the help of other teachers in our efforts.

The result of our work is the present book, which we hope has done several things. First and foremost, we hope that this book has allowed you to continue developing closer and more professional relationships with parents. We also hope that our book has helped you to value parents as the "knowledgeable others" that they truly are. In writing this book, we have presented a set of questions that you can use in many ways. These questions can serve as a beginning point for gaining information, they can be adapted and modified to suit your specific needs and concerns, and they can be asked at different points throughout the year in order to create a picture of students' home lives that can be increasingly clarified. In addition to these questions, we have also developed different strategies in order to help you think conceptually and reflectively about the information you have collected about the children that you tend to "worry about." Most importantly, we have aspired to give you a tool and a mechanism for thinking about who the children are that you teach and what you can do to connect home and school literacies.

We, as authors, recognize that teachers are often privy to lots of information about the homes of the students they teach, but we feel that oftentimes teachers have not had access to a way to purposefully and constructively gain information from parents and use it to benefit students in the classroom. With this in mind, we have attempted to clear a path for you that will lead you to better understandings of both parents and children. Our journey or "path" does not end with this book, and neither does yours. We don't believe that our book provides an endpoint or a complete solution to the problems inherent in establishing positive interactions and communication between parents and teachers—but we do believe that it gets us closer. Our challenge to you is to begin where we have left off, to "join hands with us," and to continue to pass the word to other educators about *A Path to Follow.*

"May the force be with you" and keep you on the path toward opening successful lines of communication with families and children, especially those families and children who most need to be heard and understood.